Performance Is Key

Performance Is Key

Connecting the Links to Leadership and Excellence

Vincent F. Cotter and Robert D. Hassler

ROWMAN & LITTLEFIELD
Lanham • Boulder • New York • London

Published by Rowman & Littlefield
A wholly owned subsidiary of
The Rowman & Littlefield Publishing Group, Inc.
4501 Forbes Boulevard, Suite 200, Lanham, Maryland 20706
https://rowman.com

Unit A, Whitacre Mews, 26-34 Stannary Street, London SE11 4AB, United Kingdom

Copyright © 2018 by Vincent F. Cotter and Robert D. Hassler

All rights reserved. No part of this book may be reproduced in any form or by any electronic or mechanical means, including information storage and retrieval systems, without written permission from the publisher, except by a reviewer who may quote passages in a review.

British Library Cataloguing in Publication Information Available

Library of Congress Cataloging-in-Publication Data

Includes bibliographic references.
ISBN 978-1-4758-4016-2 (cloth : alk. paper)
ISBN 978-1-4758-4017-9 (pbk. : alk. paper)
ISBN 978-1-4758-4018-6 (electronic)

∞ ™ The paper used in this publication meets the minimum requirements of American National Standard for Information Sciences Permanence of Paper for Printed Library Materials, ANSI/NISO Z39.48-1992.

Printed in the United States of America

Contents

Foreword · vii
Preface · ix
Introduction · xiii

I: The Essential Elements
1. Alignment · 3
2. An Achievement-Focused Attitude · 11
3. Accountability · 17
4. Aptitude for Adept Leadership · 23

II: Assessing the Foundation of High-Performing Schools
5. Organizational Reflection · 33

III: Reaching for Higher Performance
6. Making Schools and Districts High Performing · 43
7. Planning for Success · 55
8. Strategies for Success · 63
9. Case Studies · 75

Conclusion · 91

IV: Appendixes
Appendix A: Activity Worksheets · 101
Appendix B: School Systems Cross-Check · 133

Appendix C: My One-Page Plan	151
Appendix D: Master-Teacher Program	155
Notes	157
Bibliography	163
About the Authors	167

Foreword

Few leaders in the United States can claim high and continuously improving student achievement, positive morale and supportive staff, and the trust and confidence of parents and the larger local community. Authors Vincent F. Cotter and Robert D. Hassler make such bold claims in *Performance Is Key*. For my part, I have concluded that, based on my experience over the last thirty years, the swagger is justified. Let me highlight why I've come to this conclusion.

Perhaps the best way to unpack their design is to examine the critical elements to high performance. First, the leader's intense passion for the "learning for all" mission is the apparent fuel that served to supercharge the entire journey with all its complexities. Second, in a variety of different ways, the leader's passion was multiplied through different forms of involvement of staff and community. Third, these leaders nurtured the policy support of their respective school boards. The passion of continuous improvement took the form of a contagion in the communities.

Energy released without a clear focus can quickly dissipate or, even worse, be destructive. Furthermore, highly efficient deployment of the limited human and financial resources was one of the essential components to the success of these leaders. Aligning the intent, the teaching, and the assessments proved to be the "power train" of the design.

The efficient use of scarce resources demands choosing tactics and strategies that represent proven practices. Building on the proven practices of those who have gone before is a rare commitment among today's leaders. The design is built on research and proven practices. These leaders know that nothing is more empowering than evidence of a payoff for the effort. They also recognize that everyone must have skin in the game.

Needless to say, these leaders lived in the arena of accountability but realized that a hands-on approach, with ownership for district direction, was the only way to create the cultural changes necessary for real improvement.

For these reasons, these leader-authors are justified in walking among their professional peers and colleagues with swagger. They truly have narrowed the focus of creating higher-performing schools to critical key elements that, if implemented as designed, will place your school on the path to improvement.

What makes the design unique is that the process identifies the disconnections in a school, district, or organization. These authors encourage, inspire, and motivate leaders not only to focus on performance but also to utilize the strategies and practices in implementing the Essential Elements to reach higher performance. The authors argue that the time is now to begin the journey beyond the status quo toward higher-performing schools. I wholeheartedly agree!

Dr. Larry W. Lezotte
Michigan State University
Effective Schools
Author
Council of Chief School State Officers' Distinguished Service Award
Brock International Prize in Education

Preface

IMAGINE! BELIEVE! ACT!

It was once said that for anything to happen, you would need to imagine it.

Take a moment to reflect on what can happen if you not only imagine it but also believe it—and then act on proven leadership strategies to harness all aspects of your school or district to ensure that your district is poised to become high performing.

Imagine high-performing schools where

- 90 percent of all students are proficient in reading and mathematics on local, state, and national assessments
- student achievement has increased by over 50 percent within a five-year period
- student proficiency has improved every year for more than ten consecutive years
- achievement gaps have closed dramatically for all student subgroups
- advanced-placement participation has increased by 200 percent over a five-year period
- a larger percentage of AP students have obtained advance college standing
- disciplinary referrals and suspensions are reduced
- students are graded on clearly articulated outcomes and genuine learning
- students are exposed to high-level content and activities that require higher-level thinking
- students take active leadership roles in their learning and work collaboratively in formulating questions, initiating topics, and participating in discussions

- classrooms intellectually engage students through well-designed learning tasks that require complex thinking
- students present projects, utilize technology, and write creatively
- a majority of students take an advanced-placement course
- more than 90 percent of the school's graduates continue their education
- collaborative leadership and professional-learning communities are fostered
- and teachers with exemplary skills demonstrate a strong commitment to the success of all students by providing rigorous learning opportunities, providing constructive daily feedback, and accommodating various student-learning styles.

As former superintendents, we experienced these dramatic successes and now as consultants to schools and colleges we see pockets of this type of educational success. However, more often than not, a number of districts that are not only struggling but also not achieving have become frustrated with their lack of progress and have lost hope.

Far too many schools and districts have come to believe that the variables, influences, and external challenges are too great to overcome. This type of thinking stifles the improvement that we know can be attained by any school or district despite the challenges that they may face. We believe that it is possible to achieve excellence. It may just take longer to get there, but it is possible.

Educators are by nature well-intentioned. Most school districts work hard to develop strategic plans and implement required initiatives designed to improve student learning, all the while struggling to get the most out of each declining funding dollar. However, the execution of these plans and reforms often fall short of the intended results. We believe that it is possible to soar to high-performing levels by establishing a set of proven steps by developing

- a results-based culture through organizational alignment
- a collaborative, supportive organizational attitude
- a comprehensive stakeholder-driven accountability model
- and an emphasis on adept leaders with the requisite skills to create high-performing environments in which students thrive and succeed.

These steps will provide a continuous-improvement culture that ensures initiatives, programs, and strategies are aligned and designed to attain the desired results.

Many schools and districts implement improvement plans but fall short of the desired outcomes by failing to recognize the nuances and subtleties in the improvement process. We believe that this design and easy-to-follow method will assist schools and districts in developing implementation strategies critical to building a collaborative, inclusive process, but we also recognize the importance of leadership, particularly central office leaders, who are central to facilitating such a process.

While it is often convenient for politicians and other groups to place any failures and shortcomings of US schools at the feet of educators in general, we believe that, what with with the myriad of proposed solutions and pressures from a variety of sources to implement some questionable reforms and practices, the failure to make dramatic gains in student achievement are a lack of focus on and attention to four critical elements in the schools: we have personally witnessed a lack of fundamental leadership regarding *alignment, attitude, accountability*, and *adept leadership*. This book attempts to narrow the process of becoming a high-performing school by addressing these four critical elements. This publication also provides the philosophy essential to understanding the importance of these critical elements, poses reflective questions for school leaders, and offers concrete strategies to begin the process of creating a framework for excellence.

Even with the creation of a framework for excellence based on the critical areas of alignment, achievement based on attitude, accountability, and a positive, adept leadership, a variety of concrete and more subtle process components are tangential and coincide with the implementation of the four identified critical elements to high-performing schools.

Based on our experiences, we know that with a rigorous curriculum, the appropriate methodology, and a dedicated staff all schools can become bastions of academic growth and begin the journey to higher performance. We know if you personalize the student environment and fortify it with a backbone of high expectations, success is possible. It is also recognized that change is a process, which requires the execution of an achievement plan over a period of time.

Change and improvement can be difficult but are certainly not impossible. They are within the grasp of every school and district, but more important is how change occurs and how it aligns with the targeted goals. Every school and district can attain high performance levels without purchasing expensive new programs, textbooks, and the latest "cutting-edge" curriculum materials. It simply requires an aligned focus on achievement, a "roll-up-the sleeves" mentality, and the will to get it done.

Despite the extensive research on the importance of collaboration in the improvement process, many administrators avoid it. In order for a culture to shift its focus to higher student performance, leaders must be cognizant to embed collaborative processes into the alignment and accountability steps so that action plans are understood, roles are delineated, outcomes are measured, and these steps foster a positive organizational attitude that will drive the school or district toward higher performance. Finally, adept leaders must be willing to reflect on their leadership style, be willing to discard ineffective leadership practices, and be willing to implement our proven set of steps and practices, which will guarantee a successful path in the implementation of continuous-improvement strategies.

We know that it will take courage, clarity of purpose, an unwavering belief system, and a leadership style that is both strategic and collaborative. In *Performance Is Key*, we will guide you through the steps to reach higher performance levels for your school or district and highlight the keys to success that seem to elude many well-intentioned leaders. You, too, can benefit from our seventy years of collective experience and utilize the strategies that have worked not only in our schools but also in those that sought our assistance.

We dare you not only to imagine but also to believe that it can happen and to act as an adept leader who strategizes, analyzes, and inspires your team to implement the highlighted four critical elements to become a high-performing school.

In this book, each chapter will provide an explanation as to why the highlighted component is essential when integrated into the fabric of a school district. You will also be provided with a reflection section that will pose questions, ask you to reflect on the current status of key factors, and challenge you to assess your district. Next, we will offer a series of concrete strategies and activities that we have found to be successful in our continuous-improvement efforts.

Effective leaders learn from one another and find ways to modify these insights to fit their unique circumstances. But, remember, regardless of the insights and strategies that are utilized, it is a journey of processes and incremental gains that requires savvy and adept leadership. It is also a journey that requires a school leader to maintain a no-excuses mentality. You can utilize this book and move from chapter to chapter or focus on those areas that you feel are most critical to you. However, we feel that each of the elements must be addressed to attain the greatest impact for your school.

Introduction

Over the last twenty years, the country's frustration with underperforming, mediocre, and failing schools has grown and most recently reached a crescendo of deafening proportion. Almost on a daily basis, the issue of student achievement and how to "fix" the problem of poor performance along with the methods of how to accomplish it comes under furious debate in some sectors of the country. The federal government, legislators, and governors have responded to desperate parental voices by implementing a variety of well-intentioned "silver-bullet" solutions that are mere Band-Aids to the issue. Most of these suggested solutions lack the substance or science to create real positive outcomes in the lives of children.

Even with $4.5 billion spent on reforms, initiatives, and incentives for the "Race to the Top"[1] fund, overall student performance on the National Assessment of Educational Progress and the Program for International Student Assessment remains stagnant.[2] The overall failure to move schools forward despite such investment is discouraging to all community members, professionals in the field, students, and parents and at the same time is perplexing to all those impacted by such results.

Despite these performance indicators, we believe that the resolution of underperformance ultimately remains with the leadership of a school or district and with the leader's ability to effectively articulate and collaboratively execute a vision and to align a variety of factors associated with that vision to create high-performing schools. Imagine driving a car with bad wheel alignment or one with misfiring spark plugs. Beyond being inefficient, the car's performance is substandard and will never reach its peak performance without the expertise of a skilled technician.

Much like the car needs a mechanic, our schools need leaders with the ability to assess the functionality of an organization, analyze a variety of data points, and exercise judgment in aligning the organization for high-performing outcomes. Even with the best facilities, exemplary technology, and dedicated teachers, no commodity is as valuable as adept leadership, which can produce the desired results.

Adept leadership provides the framework to connect the dots that aligns all aspects of the organization for maximum performance. It is visionary leadership that sets the tone, creates the expectations, communicates the goal, and collaborates within the parameters of a collaborative framework that transcends the minutiae and the politics plaguing substantive growth. These practices, which can be learned and duplicated, are found in our book.

With schools and districts on the brink of losing public confidence due to their failure to improve student performance levels and their inability to comprehensively execute strategic plans, the excuse or victim mentality can no longer be tolerated. Funding, demographics, lack of programs, and insufficient parental involvement are often cited as factors in failing schools. While these factors are very powerful to those attempting to explain the school's failures despite very good intentions, in reality there is no excuse for districts that are at the minimum of acceptable functionality and not improving in any substantive way. There is an abundance of research to indicate that we have the knowledge to put into place those processes and strategies that will improve current performance and to continue to work on creating not only good but great schools.

While as a nation our results are not what we desire, there are examples similar to the successes of 90/90/90 schools—where 90 percent percent of the students are classified as low income, 90 percent are minority, and 90 percent meet or exceed district and state academic standards.[3] Despite the challenges and obstacles to success, these schools have demonstrated that the answers to success are not found in proprietary programs or purchased curriculum materials. Rather, these schools focused on analyzing and improving academic achievement by identifying best instructional practices. These practices are clearly replicable without the addition of extraordinary resources. But the work is not easy.

Effective Schools founder Larry Lezotte has warned that "this work is not for the faint of heart."[4] Many of the previously cited reasons for failure are often considered beyond our direct control. Lamentations like, "If only we had more funding," "If only I could group students the way I wanted," "If only I had better students," or "If only parents took more responsibility" merely bemoan failure.

These excuses never focus on what *we*, the leaders and educators, can accomplish together to improve our schools using the existing resources, staffing, and knowledge already internally available with our schools. The path to higher performance begins with collective reflection grounded in the four essential elements—alignment, attitude, accountability, and adept leadership. It begins with understanding what is holding us back—an understanding of the disconnections between and within the links to higher performance.

To paraphrase Jim Collins in *Good to Great*, we don't have great schools principally because we have focused on making them good enough.[5] For too many reasons we have accepted the status quo as the norm.

Recently, while discussing the dilemma of failing schools at a state capital with a leader on "turnaround schools," it was expressed that if the schools at the local level knew how to change the direction of the schools, they would have already done it.

Having noted the accomplishments of the 90/90/90 schools, we reject this logic. Rather, we endorse Ron Edmunds's belief that "we already know more than we need" in order to do it and that "we can, whenever and wherever we choose to, successfully teach all children."[6]

With so many schools in state receivership for so many years with additional layers of state oversight and additional funding, it might be logical for a state department leader to develop such a response. Instead, it singles out a glaring failure of leadership. Either the leadership doesn't know how to change the course, or they lack the will to do so. In the end, the good-enough approach prevails, and this language is couched in the rhetoric of failure.

In reality, the good-enough approach is not enough for students to succeed locally, regionally, or, certainly, globally. Unfortunately, this mind-set has resulted in some schools and districts being ranked in performance only slightly above some third-world countries.[7] The status quo or maintenance approach will result in too many unfulfilled promises and untapped student potential. I know that it wasn't good enough for my children, my school, or my district!

School board members, superintendents, parents, and teachers need to ask the question if it's good enough for them! If it's not, begin the journey to excellence with us now.

NOTES

I

The Essential Elements

For schools and districts to reach a higher level of performance, there are essential elements that must be part of their fabric for improvement to occur and for it to be sustainable. This section identifies those elements and provides examples of schools, businesses, and military bodies that have been successful in reaching a higher level of performance.

Chapter One

Alignment

IMAGINE

Whether you are new to education or an experienced educator, close your eyes, and imagine the full potential of your school or district. What would it look like? How do you envision the students entering the school? What does instruction in the classroom look like?

Now envision the interaction between student and teacher. As a leader, how do you see yourself? How do you want others to see you? How do parents view the school? How do students view the school? How does staff interact with the parents? Many, many more questions . . .

Great athletes and musicians have always envisioned their performances, from beginning to end. They envision every detail with vivid accuracy prior to its execution. This reflection intensifies one's focus and increases the potential for strong outcomes. Reflection can make the difference between success and failure, mediocrity or excellence.

It was the day before Labor Day. The building was a nondescript concrete structure in a bleak section of the city. In an aloof manner, the principal assigned me a room and gave me a class list. He provided directions to the room, reminded me of the department and faculty meeting within the next two hours, and offered a parting "Good luck."

The room was located up a graffiti-strewn staircase and down a long, dark hallway. It was larger than the normal classroom but absent furniture, books, a clock, closet, etc. It was a room and not much more. What with no materials and furniture, the principal advised me to search the building for what was needed. Several routine meetings later, the search began. Students were arriving in a few days. There were IEPs to check and furniture and materials to find.

Over the weekend that followed, I envisioned what was needed and what the students deserved. The students were going to arrive regardless of the conditions. It was up to me and me alone to make it happen. The remainder of the weekend was spent buying supplies, developing assessments from scratch, and strategizing where to locate materials. The free library provided books; a desk here and a desk there were quietly reallocated. Furniture was found in other rooms. Piece by piece, the vision became a reality.

Twenty-four years later, the challenge was equally great. Appointed superintendent of an underperforming school district, the Board of Education's mandate was clear: Improve student achievement. *Equally clear was that failure was not an option. Complicating the situation was a fractured school board/teacher relationship, compounded by narratives of poor teacher performance and merit pay that had become a flash point in the negotiation process.*

The district was a tangled web of layered programs, distrust, and poor student performance. Within five years, district achievement improved and continuous improvement was the norm.

Sixteen years later, two very different districts sought assistance—both high poverty and low achieving. The achievement barometer had been frozen for years, and the only solution on the horizon was a state takeover. Where to begin?

Certainly the solutions to the classroom scenario, the challenge to the superintendent, and now the two struggling districts are unique unto themselves. Each of the scenarios was complicated and simple at the same time. All required reflection and imagination.

Simply close your eyes and imagine what is possible in your school. Envision what you want each student to learn, how they would ideally learn, how you could prepare them for success, and what the outcome of their learning looks like. And before opening your eyes, mentally survey the reality of what exists.

The difficult part is when you open your eyes and plan to make it happen. Whether scanning an empty classroom without materials or having a gauntlet thrown at your feet by a school board, it would be easy to freeze with anxiety at the task at hand, but failure is not an option either for a teacher or a leader.

The real challenge for me was aligning a vision for the class with that of the school or the district. Surely my students upon arriving to class weren't expecting excellence, but it was only excellence that could overcome years of neglect. The board that had hired me as superintendent and later consultant wanted the ordinary to become extraordinary.

Finding excellence began with planning, alignment, experimentation, and execution. Success did not happen overnight, but it did begin with a design and a plan that aligned the vision and the dream. Simply put, imagination is a gift.

Imagination lifted me and helped me to understand what was possible. But imagination without a real design only results in an unfulfilled dream. A real dream begins with a plan, and a real plan begins with alignment. In many cases it might require just a few tweaks to the plan or understanding the nuances and subtleties to the improvement process but it is essential to find the missing ingredients that will maximize student potential.

ORGANIZATIONAL ALIGNMENT

Have you been part of plans, initiatives, programs, and models that have delivered the intended results? We have! In fact, all educational leaders have. We not only can help eliminate these instances that have not but also assist you in focusing on the areas that will ensure that you attain the high performance you are seeking.

In order to maximize the resources and human capital in an organization and transform it into one capable of achieving academic success for all students and one that provides a solid foundation aligning intended goals with practices, processes, and strategies, it is necessary to harness the talents of everyone in a district. This foundation is developed through a process called *organizational alignment*.

From our experience, districts believe that having a strategic plan in place is sufficient, but many times the nuances of working to achieve these goals are the culprit in failing to attain the desired results.

Organizational alignment creates the environment in a district where the central office, each school, and all stakeholders are rowing in the same direction. By ensuring that all staff members work to correlate with the vision, mission, and goals in an aligned manner, the organization will be positioned to effectively execute its initiatives and deliver the intended results.

By ensuring that the stakeholders in the community are also aligned to the direction and goals of the district, the acquisition of the necessary support and resources will be expedited to assist in sustaining the work that was taking place in every classroom. Additionally, organizational alignment must encompass all aspects of a district and school and be implemented in a consistent manner if it's to have the greatest impact on instruction and ultimately upon the students.

Without question, it is the superintendent's ability to execute the vision, mission, and strategic plans of the district and, most importantly, to allocate the resources required to do so. In turn, effective organizational alignment is also dependent on the district's senior leadership and building-level leadership to analyze its effectiveness in order to develop a plan that effectuates optimum student outcomes.

While everyone's role is critical in the implementation process, the leadership of an organization is directly responsible for its articulation and supervision and, consequently, is accountable for its student outcomes. The specific consequences of poor alignment or misalignment are directly related to underachieving schools, the misuses of resources, and the failure to develop and grow internal capacity within the organization.

For a school or district to maximize or exceed its achievement potential, all key systems and values within an organization must be integrated in a synergistic manner. If the whole is the sum of its parts, highly effective schools result from the aligned interactions and relationships between those parts.

If one of the key functions of an organization fails to operate in a synergistic manner, then the probability of the desired outcome is diminished exponentially.

All components of an organization must operate as a unified whole. Goals, plans, processes, measures, and actions must be internally consistent. Each subdivision and department must reflect the organizational beliefs, values, policies, and procedures to produce the desired outcome. Values, beliefs, and vision transcend funding, technology, and programming and should be reflected in each component of the organization.

From the highest policy makers and staff members to those entrusted to carry out the most routine daily functions, each must understand and internalize the core values of the institution. Those core values must be represented in not only how the district conducts the business of educating children but also in its goals and decision-making framework.

In the movie *Hoosiers* Gene Hackman plays a coach who inherits a dysfunctional basketball team in a community with high expectations. His basic rule, "Five passes before you can shoot," is met with great resistance. The rule requires personal internalization and great personal discipline in the development of a team in which all the components work together.[1]

An effective system requires that each person sacrifice personal self-gratification for the team's betterment, outcome, and future. "Doing your own thing" will not move a school or district toward academic achievement.

The sporting world as well as business and the military abound with examples of synergistic organizations that integrate their values into every aspect of the organization. Over twenty years ago, Tom Peters detailed exemplary business models in his acclaimed book *In Search of Excellence*, and most recently Jim Collins highlighted various corporate leaps to excellence in his highly regarded book *Good to Great*.[2] Military accomplishments are also well documented in publications and by the media.

Regardless of organizational differences, excellence rests on values, the integration of those values, and the synergistic manner in which those values drive the outcomes of the organization. A set of beliefs, if communicated and integrated into the fabric of the organization, can be utilized to assist in organizational alignment and move an organization toward excellence.

Recently the highly respected Brookings Institution reflected on the mixed results regarding "turnaround" reform efforts throughout the country.[3] Citing funding, disruption, and ineffective and flawed programs, Brookings lamented that schools leaders are reluctant to revisit this approach. Again, we suggest that these well-intentioned reforms are often doomed from the outset for a lack of continuity.

Too often school leaders seek a quick solution, a program, or a reform to solve a long-standing, complex problem such as student achievement without reexamining the institution's values, beliefs, and mission in the context of the desired outcomes.

Too often the quick fix contradicts the core values required for success or is a haphazard collection of programs without a track record of success. Most often these programs are not linked in any systemic manner and operate independently from one another.

Such was the case of a struggling urban district encountered in my capacity as a consultant. On the surface it appeared that the district had yet to encounter a program it didn't like. Their public-relations department published materials touting the district's new direction and progressive approach.

Over the years, the solution to the district's achievement problem had been to add another program until there were so many programs that the staff was somewhat confused as to what the district's instructional priorities really were. Many staff decided to go their own direction—they resorted to letting their instincts tell them what was best for their class or school.

A survival mentality kicked into place—"every man and woman for themselves." They believed in the unwritten survival philosophy: "This too shall pass." One staff actually stated that they had survived five superintendents and would survive this one too.

Unraveling this massive disconnection of purpose, program, and outcome began with collective reflection. Let's just collectively imagine what is possible. That's the beginning of alignment—reflection, introspection, and link-

ing it to where you want to go. *What are your core values, and how does that align with your instructional model?*

Failing schools often bemoan poor achievement resulting from issues associated with poverty and variables such as parental and community involvement. They feel, incorrectly, that these variables are totally beyond their control.

Failing schools often point to successful schools that have more technology, programs, and resources. A more effective approach is to introspectively reflect on the instructional variables within one's control and understand what can be done to lessen the impact of factors such as poverty and parental involvement.

There is no dispute that core values and how those values are aligned and integrated into the organization are prerequisites to success. How leaders facilitate a synergistic approach focusing all members of the organization on its outcomes is the difference between successful alignment and haphazard implementation. High-performing schools are not possible without aligning core values to targeted outcomes.

We recommend that if you think you are aligned, begin with a simple assessment—a cross section of board members, educational leaders, teachers, and parents. In the context of a school or district setting ask each what they value.

Ask each group what outcome they desire. Ask each person what the obstacles are to success or achievement. Make sure to ask the participants for evidence to support their perspective.

If there is a disconnection between values, actions, and outcomes expressed between the groups, we suggest that everyone collectively close their eyes and *imagine* what is possible; then utilize the suggested strategies in a later chapter to address the disconnections.

ESSENTIAL IDEAS

- Organizational alignment harnesses the talents of everyone in a school or district to coordinate the implementation of goals, processes, and strategies.
- Effective alignment eliminates the common problems with initiatives, plans, and programs that do not deliver the intended results by applying proven and practical strategies.
- Leaders are ultimately responsible for facilitating the alignment of an organization.
- All key systems, values, and beliefs must be integrated in a synergistic manner into the fabric of the organization.

- The ability to focus all members on its outcomes is the difference between successful alignment and haphazard implementation.

Chapter Two

An Achievement-Focused Attitude

BELIEVE

Whether in the classroom or the boardroom, it is essential to identify one's beliefs prior to accepting a challenge. Those beliefs become the baseline for actions and decisions that will guide your teaching, your tenure as principal, and your leadership as superintendent. Beliefs affect attitudes and practices.

Fundamental to improving achievement are the following beliefs:

All children can learn.
Students always come first.
Failure is not an option.
We should believe in people.
Continuous improvement is worth working toward.
Nothing can take the place of good instruction.

More importantly is defining what each belief means and what it would take to make each happen. How you define those beliefs and your commitment to them will determine your legacy as a teacher, principal, or superintendent.

They were throwaway kids. Nobody wanted them—principals, teachers, and, in some cases, those entrusted to care for them. At the middle school no one believed in them. Other than behavior, no one had expectations for them. No one really thought that they could learn. By high school, they had become angry and dejected, merely going through the motions—"same old, same old."

The burden of responsibility weighed heavily on me as the planning process began. Whether they realized it or not, those "throwaways" needed me to make a difference in their lives and to find a way to turn the corner.

It was a lot to expect, but I had to believe that under that exterior of toughness and misbehavior they wanted someone to believe in them. More often than not, they came to class disheveled, unprepared, and unable to wait for the day to end. But once they trusted me, and believed in me, they began to reach out for help.

They desperately wanted be smart or considered normal. It surprised them that they could actually perform in a regular classroom . . . do well on a quiz or a test. Beliefs and believing when linked to the skills needed for success are transformational.

A similar but different situation involved a school district years later.

The teachers operated independently. They were angry, isolated, and skeptical of efforts involving collaboration and inclusion. There was a great deal of confusion regarding practice and procedures. They were unsure as to what made a difference.

The system did not reflect a set of beliefs, so the leadership and the teacher beliefs reflected a continuum of excuses and variables that were obstacles to instruction.

Building a belief system that focused on children, one that embraced continuous improvement and accountability, was a challenge, but taking this step was a turning point to improving instruction. Five years later, the confusion dissipated, practice was focused, and achievement was improved.

There were many steps to success, but developing common beliefs was the beginning. The staff's endorsement of common beliefs assured that a prevailing attitude and atmosphere of success and excellence was possible.

Believing that success is possible and embracing a philosophy that "a child's success and failure begins with me" created a positive energy that permeated the students, teachers, and community. The "throwaways" and the disjointed district found their way through the confusion to not only achieve but also succeed.

The culture of an organization and its ability to reach high levels of achievement are inextricably intertwined with the attitudes and beliefs of those employed within it. The attitude and focus of the staff toward teamwork, collaboration, improvement, and any obstacles to success will dictate whether an organization is a success or failure in the context of its vision, mission, and goals.

With over 80 percent of a district's budget invested in personnel, it is critical that the district not only hire the best faculty and staff but also grow its capacity and retain them for sustainable and continuous growth. Research has consistently highlighted the importance of leadership in creating and facilitating an atmosphere of excellence in collaboration with a faculty and staff willing to reach for excellence.[1] Such was the case in planning a complex high school master schedule.

A flawless final examination schedule was essential in bringing the year to a close in an orderly fashion. With a team of seasoned high school administrators, we went about developing a schedule for a large high school. Due to the number of electives, the rotational schedule, and the advanced-placement courses there were many nuances to the exam schedule, which would take five days to execute.

After spending at least a day on the development of the plan, the leadership team expressed moderate confidence that all the nuances had been taken into consideration, but in reality we just weren't so sure. We knew that developing this schedule in isolation was a high-risk venture. Any mistake in the plan could cast a cloud over the competency of the team.

Wisely, we invited department heads and other curriculum leaders intimately familiar with course offerings to critique the plan. They welcomed the opportunity. They thoughtfully reviewed it, made suggestions, and revised it in a constructive manner. The plan was rolled out in a very collaborative manner. All endorsed it, and it went off without a hitch.

Lesson learned—inclusion and collaboration made the plan stronger and more viable.

Interestingly, nearly nine out of ten business executives (85 percent) in a 2016 survey of global human-capital trends rated engagement as an important (38 percent) or very important (48 percent) priority for their companies, but less than half indicated that they were prepared to tackle the engagement challenge.[2] Additionally, a Gallup survey finds that companies that engage employees outperform their peers by 147 percent,[3] and another study finds that engaged employees are likely to remain with an organization.[4]

As illustrated, for an organization to operate in an effective, synergistic manner, it is essential to develop a consensus focused on achievement and effectiveness from all constituency groups. When a common direction is developed, communicated, and implemented in a relatively uniform manner, student achievement, effectiveness, and productivity increase.

As discussed in the previous chapter, creating a sense of mission as well as commitment and focus to the mission is critical to an organization's success. Fundamental to executing an organization's mission is finding talented professionals with the correct attitudinal mind-set that is student-centered, along with having the ability to positively collaborate, function as a team member, and possess the aptitude to thrive in a continuously improving environment.

Building a school team with attitudinal components that align with the district's mission will not only increase effectiveness and dramatically improve student achievement but also improve the overall climate within the district and each building within it. These professionals infuse the organization with positive vibes resulting from teamwork, collaboration, and consistency of application. A positive attitude is contagious and morphs into a positive atmosphere.

Rick Barnes, former head basketball coach at the University of Texas, indicated in a recent interview that recruiting players with the attitudinal hallmarks of "unselfishness, high character, and a steeled work ethic" were the keys to the success of his team. Recruiting the right people eliminates "managing staff but rather allows the leader to focus on coaching and providing those supports necessary for improvement."[5]

Jim Collins, author of *Good to Great*, stresses placing the right people in the right seats on the bus to move the organization in the direction of excellence. In a school setting, recruitment and the hiring of staff members with the right attitude can be a game changer.

Having sat through hours of interviews trying to identify the individual with the prerequisite skills and knowledge base along with the right attitude for a position is often a daunting task. Often you only get one opportunity to get it right.

Ferreting out those with an inadequate knowledge base is a relatively simple process through a writing assessment or subject-matter test. Simulated teaching or situational-leadership scenarios can be helpful. Finding what is in the candidate's heart can be more difficult.

Candidates often know exactly what to say and what buzzwords to utilize. Rubrics and rankings are helpful, but in the end it always comes down to a gut check. Your best barometer becomes that old adage, when you feel it, you know it. Not always scientific, but often right.

Members of an ideal team believe that they are or will be making a difference in the lives of students and in implementing the vision and mission of the district but also enjoy being part of something bigger than themselves. To these individuals, it is not about salary or even the quality of the facility.

When confronted with obstacles, these individuals prefer to seek solutions. They are willing to reach out for assistance rather than work in isolation. These individuals are willing to sacrifice self-gratification for the team.

Being the best is a priority but only in the context of collaboration and teamwork. Excellence is viewed through the lens of a school or district's success rather than personal accolades and personal awards. Professional excellence is attained through constructive feedback, reflection, and targeted development.

In terms of leadership, foremost to the organization's success is a leader who possesses the attitudinal qualities to move an organization forward in a positive, constructive manner. The leader understands the big picture but has both the emotional quotient and technical ability to implement a plan of continuous improvement.

Not only does the leader set the tone and collaborate in establishing those parameters for success, but the leader also models, facilitates, motivates, empowers, and celebrates the success of the team. The ideal leader communicates rather than pontificates, is objective rather than subjective, and relies on a defined decision-making framework that is data-driven.

Finding a leader who has both the substance and personality to lead is often a challenge. Leaders who are very technical in nature spend a majority of their time in the compliance domain and rarely emerge as leaders with a vision for the future. Some may meet the challenge of moving beyond the status quo but often have difficulty communicating the vision. These individuals require a support team that excels in areas in which the leader is not comfortable.

On the other hand, leaders who rely on personality require other support members who are more technical. To effectively lead an organization, a leader needs to build confidence in charting a course for the future along with the ability to motivate others.

One of the most remarkable examples of teamwork, collaboration, and leadership is the US Navy's Blue Angels. The foundation to the Blue Angels' success is a basic precept: "attitude equals altitude."[6]. From the outset the Blue Angels build their team around shared values. The team's values must align with its purpose, mission, and actions. Sacrificing individual gain for the team's greater good is an essential component for maximum performance. Each member of the team is valued regardless of position and empowered to participate in making each performance better.

The leadership of the Blue Angels is transparent and lead by positive example. These leaders embrace the power of teamwork and seek to utilize the strengths that all members bring to the team. To accomplish the team's mission, honest and clear feedback keeps the team focused and contributes to delivering a consistent performance. By dealing with issues immediately, the team reinforces the concept of continuous improvement and takes a step closer to excellence. "Synergy only happens when qualified people align to a common objective."[7]

For a school leader, finding the best and brightest team members initially begins with outreach to the best colleges and universities, but researching a university's track record of successful placement is critical. Take the time to track the collegiate history of your current stars—you will be surprised!

Recognize that you want to hire staff members who not only have been exposed to the methodologies and strategies that will complement the district's quest for excellence but also possess a can-do attitude and a collaborative mind-set. Actively recruit individuals from 90/90/90 districts, which have maximized student achievement despite a variety of obstacles.

Resilient individuals embrace feedback from experienced staff because they want to be the best and contribute positively to the team. They often provide a diverse opinion because they bring to the table experiences much different than those of staff currently in the district or school.

Recognize that attitude truly does equal altitude and that the district can fill experiential gaps in the newly hired staff with the proper in-house training and staff development. Additionally, a school and district must philosophically embed the key attitudinal characteristics for success into the hiring process and at the same time ensure that each individual also possesses the technical knowledge to maximize student potential.

A high-performing school is only possible with an excellent staff, which begins with the hiring process and is nurtured through aligned professional development. Hire only the best, and move the existing fence-sitters with compelling data and a supervisory/evaluation program linked to high-performing outcomes. The culture of the organization will simply be determined by the attitude of the staff and its leadership.

ESSENTIAL IDEAS

- The culture of an organization and its ability to reach high levels of achievement are intertwined with the attitudes and beliefs of those employed within it.
- Understanding and identifying an organization's beliefs is critical, because those beliefs shape its decision making, actions, and leadership.
- Effective leadership goes well beyond establishing the vision of an organization and is dependent on the leader's ability to model, facilitate, and empower its members to work collaboratively to achieve the goals of the organization.
- Recruiting and identifying professionals with a positive attitudinal mind-set increases organizational focus and effectiveness.
- Understanding that staff members' satisfaction and the culture's perspective toward teamwork, collaboration, and improvement, along with how it resolves obstacles and roadblocks, will dictate whether an organization is a success or failure in the context of its vision, mission, and goals.
- The extent to which a school or district effectively focuses on achievement parallels its level of performance.

Chapter Three

Accountability

Standing in front of three hundred high school teachers can be intimidating. The teachers shuffled into a steeply tiered auditorium. Taking strategically located seats, by department, provided teachers with a certain level of comfort. Union representatives talked in a corner of the room. Some teachers immediately started grading papers, while others gazed some thirty feet above the principal in the steeply sloped room.

It all appeared routine to them, but today's meeting was going to be different. The message that they were about to hear was going to go down hard. They were accustomed to accolades. They were a Blue Ribbon School. They were comfortable with their practice. They considered themselves to be consummate professionals.

They were soon to realize that the world in which they operated was about to change. The data were clear: We were a Blue Ribbon School on the surface, but only based on very superficial criteria . . . number of classrooms, teacher degrees, books in the library, etc. The data portrayed an underachieving school . . . the top students, those identified as gifted or those taking high-level courses, were doing well, but the middle-level students were not achieving.

A belief that outcomes for learning are the responsibility of the students and parents was deeply entrenched at all levels. They failed to conceive that student failure could be related to their practice. They were clear that there were other reasons for underperformance. They were angry and felt disrespected. They believed that they were right.

Changing this entrenched philosophy on learning was going to require a shift in beliefs and a framework of accountability for learning and instruction. Everyone had to be accountable for student achievement—the board, the administration, and the teachers. How we delivered instruction and our responsibility for those results had to change.

It was a formidable challenge, and it began with one question—Why? Followed by a second—How? The why was easy—we were not serving all students. The how was much more complicated.

Accountability has become the buzzword in the educational-reform movement. In an effort to stem the tide of mediocrity and underperformance on a global level, education reformers have called for accountability systems that mirror approaches often found in the business world. Teacher organizations have reacted to the business bottom-line models, arguing that students are not widgets and that a variety of variables—many of which are beyond their control—impact student outcomes.

While understanding the merit of both the business model—often termed the "real world"—and the rebuttals by educators of such systems, we believe that real accountability in education is necessary if excellence and real-world outcomes are the objective but recognize that these systems will only be effective if collaboration and professional growth are factored into the equation.

Researchers say more often the evaluation process is perfunctory because there are no agreed upon norms for what constitutes good listening.[1]

Without question, when it comes to creating and implementing a system of accountability, the devil is in the details, but those details must include a structure that aligns the values, mission, and goals in a collaborative manner that is results-oriented. It is essential that all components of the organization dovetail toward its focus and that its processes also reflect its targeted outcomes.

To compete at a higher level, an organization must define its benchmark indicators relative to high-performance outcomes, have systems in place to reach those outcomes, and have the ability to continuously monitor and adjust its operation to attain its goals. By incorporating the key components into a school or district system of accountability along with essential strategies for implementing such a system, a school leader must have the ability to design an accountability framework that will collaboratively launch the district toward excellence.

Without a comprehensive and collaborative accountability system led by a school leader, preferably the superintendent, no district will be able to achieve their desired results. By integrating a continuous-improvement model into a robust accountability system, an organization's progress toward goal attainment will be measured through clear and objective indicators.

Overall, despite a national perception that educators are reluctant to embrace accountability, we have witnessed educator support for results-oriented accountability systems that are inclusively developed, collaborative in design, and supportive. Accountability programs that are arbitrary and capricious are doomed for failure, because they are often void of collaboration and opportunities for growth.

We believe that a results-oriented system must include all departments, groups, and individuals by setting collaborative targets aligned to the goals of the organization. A culture of accountability must be developed and nourished throughout the district, beginning at the superintendent level. An effective system addresses all facets of the organization, including both the instructional side and the operational-support divisions.

A beginning point for the organization is to complete the necessary work of aligning each department to the vision of the district. The vision paints a graphic picture of what is envisioned.[2] Measurable goals based on the vision are developed by departments, providing an accountability framework for the entire district. Most importantly, however, is an ongoing review of progress based on multiple sources of data. Optimally, this review should take place on a monthly basis.

Today schools and districts for the most part establish measurable goals as part of a strategic plan, a mandate from the state or internal initiatives. Again, it is the nuance of the interconnection between alignment and accountability that requires attention. What is measured, how it is measured, and how often the review takes place make the difference in high-performing school districts.

Many districts do not establish an accountability system that holds everyone accountable from the superintendent down through every level of the organization on a monthly basis. This monthly review provides an opportunity to assess progress and adjust the plan accordingly if necessary. Without a monthly review, those designated to implement goals are often prone to procrastination and lack of execution.

The one-page plan that I elaborate on in appendix C[3] is an excellent tool for conducting the monthly review, but it is the process that the district utilizes to establish goals, action plans, and follow-up that matters most. Instructional walk-throughs also provide an opportunity to discuss goal progress.

A monthly or quarterly review process maintains the organization's momentum. This review process requires an organization to maintain a constant focus on progress and to ensure that goals are being carried out as designed.

With the utilization of monthly or quarterly data in the context of goal progress and benchmark analysis, the organization becomes nimble and flexible enough to adjust to data trends and to adjust its strategy to immediately remediate any detected deficiencies. This process brings each goal to life and becomes a daily focus for all members of the organization.

Envision an umbrella with data raining down; the umbrella's spokes consists of standards, assessment, staff development, expectations for learning, policies, and procedures. Depending on the direction of the data, the leadership can tilt the handle to make the necessary accommodations.

If a monthly or quarterly review process is not utilized, much of the data runs off the umbrella, and opportunities for adjustments are lost. Often these accommodations result in regrouping and reteaching concepts or adjustments in instructional techniques and methodology that may have potentially created achievement gaps. On the operational side, process and practices can be altered to improve efficiency and effectiveness, thereby saving valuable resources.

Beyond the process of district-, building-, and departmental-goal measurement and review, a critical component to an accountability system is evaluation. As part of this accountability system, and most importantly in becoming a high-performance system, an evaluation system ensuring the delivery of quality instruction is critical.

In research conducted in Tennessee, Sanders and Rivers demonstrate the importance of quality instruction. Over a multiyear period, Sanders focused on the impact that high-performing and low-performing teachers had on student achievement.[4]

Furthermore, Tucker and Stronge discovered that when third-grade children were placed with highly rated mathematics teachers for three consecutive years, the students scored in the range of fifty-two percentile points higher in math at the conclusion of fifth grade compared to other third graders who had been placed with lower-rated teachers for those three consecutive years.[5] Sanders and Rivers's research has led to the commonly held belief that the single greatest determinant to learning is not the variables associated with socioeconomic levels or funding but, rather, instruction.[6]

Other researchers have found that teaching has six to ten times as much impact on achievement as all other factors combined of specified but examples are class size, new programs, and funding.[7] It is further noted that improving a teacher's overall classroom practices by a fraction can improve student performance by one-seventh of a standard deviation in reading and one-tenth of a standard deviation in math.[8]

This research highlights our belief that an effective collaborative evaluation system must be in place for a district or school to become high performing. We further believe that while the new rubric-designed systems offer great promise in improving instruction, many districts have not developed the associated processes connected to the evaluation system to realize improved instruction and, in turn, the promise of increased student achievement.

An evaluation system must connect with the district's overarching goal of providing higher performance outcomes, and, therefore, it must align with the district's vision, goals, and performance targets. For an evaluation plan to integrate with the district's accountability plan, it must ensure that

- the proper awareness has been developed with all stakeholders
- the philosophy and culture of collaboration is established through the organization
- the follow-up and processes are established to ensure consistency of design implementation
- and measures are implemented to determine how effectively the evaluation is implemented.

Obviously, the quality of instruction determines the effectiveness in how the curriculum is being delivered to the students. If the curriculum is rigorous, relevant, and twenty-first-century-based, a fairly reliable hypothesis might predict the attainment of designated goals; but in reality methodological consistency through professional collaboration is often the difference between success and failure, achievement and underachievement.

Finally, often neglected in most accountability schemes for schools is a system that recognizes existing and emerging talent by providing opportunities for leadership. Master-teacher programs, some in existence for over fourteen years (see case study #1, chapter 9, "Reaching above and beyond"), empower and create leaders.

Carefully designed programs of accountability include an intervention process for struggling staff that provides support through an intervention team composed of administrators, teachers, and specialized staff. Accountability systems harnessing the collective nature of educators through collective recognition at the building and department should be considered.

Two years later, the same high school faculty shuffled into the auditorium once again. This meeting included all staff . . . aides, custodians, cafeteria workers. They were unsure why the meeting had been called. Throughout the day, rumors circulated—funding cuts, a personnel update on staffing and scheduling—but it was the five-foot boxes at the front of the room that drew their attention.

It was now time to celebrate. Our students had scored extremely well on the state assessment. We had excelled with all students. Each faculty member received a school baseball cap . . . a small token of our appreciation. All groups celebrated the results and wore the hats proudly throughout the next school day. All groups had assumed responsibility for the results. All groups had embraced the culture of collective accountability.

When a school or district attempts to implement highly regarded programs of accountability in isolation and independent of the organization's structure and without consideration of its culture, the outcomes will not reflect the projected growth and will not justify the expenditure, resource allocation, or expense of human capital. In fact, this missed opportunity will make the change process much more difficult in the future.

On the other hand, an organization will thrive with a thorough and detailed alignment of district goals from the superintendent's office to the classroom, as well as in all operational-support departments, with a focus on instructional practices and a rigorous curriculum, instructional methodology, and an accountability system that emphasizes collaboration, professional growth, teamwork, and support.

Attempts to impose a business model or a perceived arbitrary and capricious accountability system have consistently failed to produce desired results. It is only through the alignment of instruction and curriculum to an accountability framework that will create an atmosphere of substantive continuous improvement and ultimately pave the way to high-performance outcomes.

ESSENTIAL IDEAS

- Real accountability in education is necessary if excellence and real-world outcomes are the objective.
- While the term *accountability* has been overused and some groups have a negative perception of it, there are key components of accountability that every district can implement immediately to improve performance.
- A system of accountability can ensure methodological consistency, which is often the difference between success and failure, achievement and underachievement.
- A system of accountability is only successful when it connects instructional outcomes to the delivery of curriculum and is operational in an atmosphere of continuous improvement.
- Evaluation is a component of a system of accountability.
- An evaluation system must connect with the district's overarching goal of providing higher outcomes.
- Benchmarking practices, developing collaborative targets, establishing a results-oriented system, and implementing an ongoing monitoring and review process are critical to establishing an effective accountability process that results in high-performing schools and districts.
- Quality evaluation systems that are both summative and formative can assist in creating quality teaching and learning environments, but implementation of those programs requires consistency and leadership.

Chapter Four

Aptitude for Adept Leadership

ACT

Leadership requires action. As basic as that sounds, more often than not educational leaders just do not lead. Some leaders lack the vision and skill to produce high-performing results. Other leaders lack the judgment, experience, and skills to know when something needs changing and when it doesn't.

Leaders need the ability to assess an environment, determine strengths and weaknesses, collaborate in the development of a plan, and execute a real plan that will make a difference. Most importantly, leaders need to be able to transfer the vision into action.

Both schools were very similar. They were concrete fortresses. No windows, no landscaping, a parking lot. They were modern-looking amid the aging row homes. They were an architect's vision of education—modern but not functional. But as much as they were alike, they were very different.

In the middle school, the instructional plan was clear . . . keep a lid on behavior. Good teaching was considered the ability to control behavior. Admittedly, keeping the kids in line was an important priority, but after establishing basic classroom behavior, there was little understanding of what constituted good instruction. We were provided a classroom set of textbooks, issued a ream of paper for the month, and given a few pencils.

There really wasn't a known vision or mission related to instruction. It was clear that you were considered "good" if you had no issues. Teachers were isolated, uncollaborative, unsupported. They were guarded and anxious. You had to find your own way, to persevere, and to teach.

Learning to teach and to have students succeed was a matter of experimentation and risk-taking. There were hard lessons learned about teaching and administration. Despite the situation, we learned about the need for collaboration, relationships, inclusion, decision making, risk-taking, and experimentation.

Several years later, I was positioned across town in a high school where I had been named part of a leadership team. The school was equally challenging, but the atmosphere was different. Controlling student behavior was important, but creativity and an instructional focus were equally so. Teachers proposed programs and were given the latitude to take risks. Career academies were implemented. Teachers were recognized for instructional excellence. Students still struggled, but supports existed to assist them.

The difference between the two schools was one of leadership. One was proactive, possessed a vision, and executed a plan for improvement. The leadership was willing to act to change the status quo. The other school was only about survival.

Leadership does make a difference, but *adept leadership* is skilled at moving schools and districts forward in reaching goals that make a difference in the lives of children. Adept leadership maximizes the potential for staff to achieve effective change and achieve high performance for *all* students. In the end, real outcomes occur when imagination, beliefs, and action intersect with the elements of alignment, atmosphere, accountability, and adept leadership.

Traditionally, schools have been layered with a variety of well-intentioned programs driven by legislators or other groups as a quick fix to complicated issues. Adept leaders cannot succumb to a silver-bullet mentality. It is not about new programs, strategies, and initiatives.

Adept leaders are not this year's "new thing" leaders but, rather, seek solutions and results. They focus on improving existing programs, increasing student achievement, and improving organizational effectiveness. Adept leaders step up and provide the guidance and direction that reinforce the beliefs and values of the organization.

Given the parameters of the school day, a leader must possess an aptitude to focus an organization on its goal of improving student achievement. Adept leaders maximize student potential by eliminating peripheral distractions and marginal programs. Adept leaders recognize that they have control over a wide range of variables during the school day and must exercise both practical and visionary judgment in moving a district or school forward along the vertical and horizontal continuum of improvement.

Even with an established framework and design for success, leaders must also recognize that flexibility in the implementation process is critical to maintaining momentum in the push for international excellence. Consensus, so long as it does not compromise the integrity of the organization's values and goals, essentially builds inclusiveness and trust. The strengths inherent in each organization should be utilized to their fullest potential within the framework of excellence to encourage risk-taking and out-of-the-box thinking.

Playing it safe often results in reinforcing the failures of the past and maintaining the status quo. Upon reflecting on the stagnation of US student-achievement scores, Arne Duncan, Secretary of Education in the Obama administration, indicates that leaders should utilize resources at the state and local levels to "drive change and reform."[1] In essence, Duncan advocates that leaders embrace Mike Schmoker's concept of teacher-conducted R&D.[2]

To fully utilize a research or experimental platform, adept leaders must possess the analytical aptitude and judgment that allows the data and their experiential intuition to guide the decision-making process. Most importantly, a leader must possess an aptitude to collaborate and engage the staff and community in the organization's mission.

All members of the organization must believe in its purpose, direction, and mission and must trust those leading it. In essence, the leader must nurture a people-centered organization. With a supportive team and a visionary leader, the children of the metaphorical village will be capable of competing at a higher level.

The people process demands that we never forget that leadership is about leading people!

Adept leaders understand the importance of positive staff morale, particularly when an organization implements a continuous-improvement model and expects higher performance. Adept leaders have communication and inclusionary decision-making skills at the top of its toolbox.

Effective adept leaders inclusively establish and communicate clear direction for their district and school. Even though it takes a great deal of effort to successfully execute and achieve the intended results, adept leadership recognizes that the goals of the district and school cannot be achieved in isolation.

Engaging internal and external stakeholders is a critical practice in a school of excellence. When common direction and consensus is established with input and work from staff and the community, districts and schools can dramatically improve their results. When resources, budget, personnel, and the community are well aligned to achieve the target goals, productivity and effectiveness increase.

EXECUTION

Realize that execution is a leader's foremost responsibility!

Peter Block calls all school leaders to action, insisting that "there is *no excuse* for leadership that fails to improve learning for *all* students." Block says, "We need to stop asking how. We now have the knowledge, the skills, the methods, the tools, the capacity, and the freedom to do whatever is required to serve all students well. All that is needed is the will and courage to choose to move on."[3]

One of the most important responsibilities of a leader is executing the vision and mission of the organization. In *The New Gold Standard*, Joseph Michelli says that, "no matter what the nature of the business, a company's leadership is always tasked with making the vision come alive on the front line."[4] While developing a quality plan is job number one, executing the plan is very close behind. Unfortunately, many leaders spend too much time on the development of the strategy and not enough time executing it.

Bossidy and Charan observe that "strategic plans often did not work in practice. Leaders placed too much emphasis on what some call high-level strategy, on intellectualizing and philosophizing, and not enough on implementation. A familiar scenario is that a team agrees on a project or initiative and then nothing happens. No company can deliver on its commitments or adapt well to change unless all leaders practice the discipline of execution at all levels."[5] If the discipline of execution is not modeled at the executive level, then it surely will not be evident throughout the organization.

We have found that execution is an issue with many of our clients. In most cases, the clients have articulated a strategic plan with measurable goals and have identified programs or initiatives to assist them in goal attainment. However, the nuances of their execution strategy are often roadblocks to successful implementation.

Execution fails due to common issues such as developing the plan without sufficient collaboration, layering conflicting programs, and a general failure to communicate the importance of the plan and its relationship to high-performance outcomes. Successful plans are aligned with measurable goals that wend seamlessly into the fabric of the daily instructional process.

Complementing a focus on execution is the leader's ability to remove roadblocks that obstruct reaching district goals. Finding a way to assist teachers to teach and for students to learn is the mantra of servant leadership.

Robert K. Greenleaf defined the term *servant leader* as "servant first," which is "sharply different from one who is leader first." The servant leader has a "natural desire . . . to serve first," versus a leader who seeks power and position. In turn, the organization serves those attempting to reach the desired outcomes.[6] Adept leaders know how to apply this concept to allocate the resources and supports to make high performance a reality.

STAFF ENGAGEMENT

Research is clear that companies focusing on establishing programs that address staff engagement and satisfaction are more successful. Without this effort, a great percentage of employees state that they are not satisfied with their work, do not have an understanding of the organization's purpose and direction, and do not trust that the organization cares and provides the necessary information and tools to accomplish their work.

Successful companies truly are people-centered organizations. Enterprise Media offers six steps for leaders developing a people-centered organization.

1. Treat staff as a balance sheet by focusing on conditions for positive gains.
2. Create a culture that celebrates staff and brings out their best.
3. Promote business literacy.
4. Create a positive working environment.
5. Focus on staff values.
6. Achieve widespread accountability and reward services.[7]

For some reason, many districts and schools do not seem to have an understanding of the importance of creating people-centered organizations. Maybe this is because schools exist to educate students and, therefore, the focus on employee engagement and satisfaction in a district seems to get lost in the work of educating the students. Possibly it is the friction caused by management and labor vying for control over the organization or the overall political climate created by external forces attempting to build a system of accountability.

Despite this disconnection between management and labor, history has demonstrated that organizations identifying the right people and empowering them often find that issues associated with motivation and commitment are eliminated.[8] Schools can find the same success in student achievement by empowering their employees, which ensures that they are engaged and motivated.

In *The 3 Keys to Empowerment* Blanchard, Carlos, and Randolph cite the empowerment of employees as "one of the most promising but least understood concepts."[9] We have seen too many managers charge head first into attempting to engage and empower employees, only to end up really giving lip service to this area.

How to empower is perceived differently by different leaders. All too often, leaders think providing an opportunity for staff to take part in the decision-making process is sufficient to empowering them. However, we have found that key to empowerment are:

- creating more autonomy by clearly establishing boundaries for employees
- forming, training, and nurturing teams in order to flatten an organization
- and sharing information in a transparent manner.

These steps to empowerment require the ability of a leader to give up any perceived power and trust employees. However, the key to successfully implementing the three key empowerment ingredients is to provide hands-on leadership and training in each of the above-mentioned areas.

PARENT AND COMMUNITY ENGAGEMENT

Adept leaders recognize that districts and schools need to engage parents and the community to achieve high performance for *all* students. The research is clear that students achieve at their optimum achievement levels when parents are engaged in their schools.

As educators work to close achievement gaps, increase proficiency, and meet state standards, they find that one of the most cost-effective methods to doing so is to implement a parent-engagement program. Unfortunately, this proven method to increasing achievement is one of the least-utilized strategies, because it is perceived to being one of the variables in the education process most difficult to control.

Again and again, we have heard the excuse, *We can't force parents to engage in their children's education.* Again, this is a convenient excuse for schools not achieving at higher levels. Adept leaders understand that it is essential to engage parents in the education of their children.

Those districts that have developed a parent-engagement process have found instead that not only does parent engagement help districts and schools improve student achievement, it is also critical in building support to acquire the necessary resources in the development of a plan geared for success and can be achieved more easily than perceived.

Adept leaders also recognize that parent engagement is very different from parent involvement. Most schools have parents involved with school-specific committees, back-to-school nights, and fund-raising activities. However, by ensuring that a welcoming environment is established and that strategies to engage parents in their child's education are implemented, two-way communication is enhanced. When parents are included in the decision-making process, districts and schools can take advantage of this built-in resource to improve student achievement.

It should also be noted that adept leadership also defines the role of the school or organization in relation to social issues and the extent to which it develops programs and extends its resources to solve them.

As discussed extensively by Ralph Smith, senior vice president and managing director of the Campaign for Grade-Level Reading, supported by the Annie E. Casey Foundation, at a *Sarasota Herald Tribune* community forum, a social compact should be forged between the school district and various social agencies to address such concerns.[10] It was further advocated that the school or district leader provide an annual report to the community on its progress to eliminate factors such as chronic absenteeism that undermine a child's ability to achieve.

School leaders must also recognize that the vast majority of the community at large is also composed of nonparents, seniors, and those who chose to send their children to private or charter schools. Often the opinions of this group of stakeholders are not perceived as impacting the overall operation of the district because they are not considered as having a direct vested interest in the schools.

In reality this tax base is critical to obtaining support for the school or district particularly in states with school referendums. It behooves school leadership to find a way to connect with these groups within the community at large, since funding excellence might be indirectly tied to them.

Adept leadership is the key to alignment, achievement-focused attitude, and accountability, the other three of the four essential elements for school improvement. As John Conyers says, "Providing an excellent education requires an excellent organization."[11] It is our belief that without adept leadership neither will be realized.

Leading a complex organization requires a leader who is adept, flexible, and a continuous learner. No one enters a leadership position prepared to face all the challenges. Erika Andersen, a leadership coach for thirty years, says "that the single most powerful way to grow as a leader" is to "become truly self-aware."[12]

The following chapters will assist you in reflecting on your leadership and how to make your school or district a place where high performance is not only a goal but a place where it flourishes.

ESSENTIAL IDEAS

- To achieve a high-performing organization, a leader must be able to transfer a vision into action.
- Adept leaders do not succumb to a silver-bullet, quick-fix mentality.
- Adept leaders roll up their sleeves by using the data from their schools and districts along with knowledge from across the world to execute the hard work of improving performance.
- Adept leaders nurture a people-centered organization by effectively engaging all stakeholders.

- Execution of a plan for higher performance is a leader's foremost responsibility.
- Adept leaders recognize the difference between parent engagement and parent involvement and the importance of parent engagement in the improvement process.
- Adept leaders are savvy in the elimination of peripheral distractions and marginal programs along with controlling the internal variables that impact achievement.
- An excellent organization will never be realized without adept leadership.

II

Assessing the Foundation of High-Performing Schools

The following chapter on organizational reflection and appendix B's school systems cross-check instrument are designed as diagnostic prescriptive tools in the examination of the strength of each essential element and the perception between constituency groups as to the prevalence of each element in the organization.

Chapter Five

Organizational Reflection

ALIGNMENT

Time and again, research has highlighted that there isn't anything mysterious about improving performance and that we have the tools available now for leaders to improve performance. As previously cited, the 90/90/90 schools have been able to improve performance without the addition of extraordinary resources or programs.

Recently the Department of Education reported that the allocated billions spent through School Improvement Grants had no impact on achievement.[1] Based on this report, it is necessary to reflect on how schools and districts plan to address student performance and the role of leadership in doing so. This observation further supports the need to reexamine the core values of a district and how these values align with its instructional practices and the ability of the organization to execute its strategy to improve student performance.

Most educators agree that each and every school could improve, let alone reach to be high performing. Recently it was reported that high-performing and high-support reform models produce high-performing outcomes.[2]

Researchers simply questioned why this model hasn't been replicated. Again, the conclusion from the research on 90/90/90 schools strongly suggests that growth in student performance is attainable. Despite the migratory nature of the population in these schools and the growing impact of poverty, these schools continue to perform at high levels each and every year.[3]

So it begs the question: If the 90/90/90 schools can do it, can all leaders attain similar results? And how can it be accomplished?

From our perspective, prior to the development of a solution for the achievement issue, it is essential that the educator or leader begin with an in-depth examination of whether all the school and district systems and processes align with the desired outcomes of becoming a high-performing school or district. This examination begins with asking some probing questions and seeking solutions to the even more difficult answers.

If you are lucky enough to attend a regional or national conference, the real opportunity is the ability to reflect on your school or district performance. Unfortunately, the reflective period ends the moment you return to the job. The daily rigor of routines, decision making, and minutiae often halts the process. The failure to reflect and later strategize severely limits the continuous-improvement process.

Take a moment and reflect on the questions provided in the next section. There are a number of questions, but the achievement issue is complex. It will take some time to find the answer or solution. Unraveling the layers and misdirection does take time, but this process will assist in aligning programs and processes and will provide direction in the reallocation of resources to outcomes.

ACHIEVING ALIGNMENT

Begin by evaluating the quality of your school or district alignment process and effectiveness. Take a moment to individually or collaboratively reflect on the following questions.

1. Do you know the vision, mission, and core values of your district?
2. If so, have you clarified the meaning of the district's vision, mission, and core values?
3. What are the strategic goals of the district?
4. Do the strategic goals cascade throughout the district from the superintendent level to all levels of the organization?
5. How often does the central office communicate progress on the strategic goals?
6. Other than the superintendent, what other leaders assist in achieving building goals?
7. What continuous plans are currently positioned to improve the processes that support all instructional and noninstructional aspects of the organization?
8. Can you describe the day-to-day work of the district? How does this work focus on student achievement or high performance?

Organizational Reflection 35

9. Which are your most successful district-wide programs? How do these programs connect to student achievement? Why are these programs successful?
10. What issue regarding student achievement has the leadership of a district consistently communicated to its membership? What solutions to student leadership have the leadership offered? Are the solutions stand-alone initiatives or woven into the fabric of the district's schools?
11. How do you describe the focus of your district? Can you identify district activities that assist in aligning district goals to outcomes?

Since these questions may initially appear as simple and definitive, they often are very enlightening when the answers are cross-referenced to comparative peer data at the state and national levels. The answers to the questions in the following will also assist in defining the culture of the district and what evidence exists in how embedded its values are and how they align with all aspects of the organization.

12. How do you define your school or district in the context of improvement? What processes or actions demonstrate that the district operates in a continuous-improvement model?
13. What specific steps has the district implemented to demonstrate that it is a district with high expectations for student performance? What are the district's aspirations? How does the district communicate its expectations? Where are the expectations embedded in the belief system of the district?
14. How are the district's achievement data connected to its practices and its planning process?

To further examine organizational values, consider defining *student achievement*, *expectations*, *inclusiveness*, *decision making*, and *empowerment* in the context of creating a high-performing school or district. Key operational words should also be examined for functionality. Finally, in the area of alignment, ask how often organizational values are reinforced and communicated.

AN ATTITUDE FOCUSED ON HIGH PERFORMANCE

Have you ever implemented an initiative that seems perfectly logical to you? Or have you ever had to implement a district initiative? As a leader you schedule the necessary conferences and training and so on. You believe that everyone is on the same page . . . but something is missing.

The implementation process is slow. There appears to be some reluctance to endorse or embrace it. Do the staff believe in the initiative? Do staff reflect the values necessary for it to be successful? Do staff believe that the change is necessary? Is it just this program, this initiative, or something bigger?

REMEMBER, ATTITUDE EQUALS ALTITUDE

To begin the process of creating an *attitude focused on high performance* and building a staff with the requisite attitudinal qualities for success, school leaders should reflect on the following.

1. Describe how the district recognizes the importance of its workforce.
2. Describe how the district provides for input into the decision-making process.
3. Describe the processes and practices that empower the staff.
4. How does the organization ensure that *all* staff members possess and demonstrate the shared values of the organization?
5. Does the school or district encourage collaboration? Have the staff been provided training on effective collaboration and problem solving? Do all members of the organization share the same definition of *collaboration*?
6. Does the school or district emphasize professional growth based on district initiatives? If so, describe the plan.
7. Describe the district's recruiting process. How does the organization ensure that new hires align with the vision of the district? How does the district get the right people on the bus? How does the organization position its staff based on their strengths?
8. How does the organization work to ensure that all members are working toward the common goals of the organization?

ACCOUNTABILITY

The union president and union representatives thought that an off-site confidential meeting would be best. They feared backlash and repercussions. The discussion topic was accountability.

The challenge was to create a system of accountability that all groups could embrace: the school board, community, parents, administrators, and teachers. There was tremendous tension resulting from a previously negotiated contract that had included an arbitrator imposing a merit-pay plan.

The plan had created a sense of distrust among groups and created a credibility gap. We needed to get it right this time. So we sat in a hotel and began to list language that could not be included in the plan.

We drafted an accountability plan of checks and balances focusing on collaboration and how this plan would improve instruction and our services.

The plan dramatically improved the district's achievement results and remains in effect today, some sixteen years later.

When a school or district attempts to implement programs of accountability in isolation and independent of the organization's structure and without consideration of its culture, the outcomes will not reflect the projected growth and will not justify the expenditure, resource allocation, and expense of capital. On the other hand, a thorough and detailed alignment of a rigorous curriculum and instructional methodology with an accountability system that emphasizes collaboration, professional growth, teamwork, and support will result in an organization that will thrive.

To begin an analysis of accountability in your school or district, reflect on the following.

1. Can you clearly identify what accountability measures have been implemented?
2. Explain how the accountability plan is collaborative.
3. Explain how all employees are included in the accountability plan.
4. How were employees prepared to participate in the devised system?
5. How is the system perceived? Does it produce the desired results or outcomes?
6. Does the system motivate and encourage collaboration?
7. What are the components to the plan?
8. Does the accountability plan include summative and formative evaluation components?
9. Does the plan include intervention and support components?
10. Describe the plan for noninstructional support services.
11. Describe the sources of data, benchmarks, and indicators of success.
12. Is the accountability system understood by members of the organization?
13. Does the system include a regularly scheduled and defined process to review the progress of the district?
14. Describe how the accountability system links results to district initiatives.
15. Describe how the results are linked to teaching and learning.
16. Describe how the results are communicated and utilized to make adjustments in the instructional and operational process.
17. Describe an academic goal that has been developed to measure student achievement.
18. What are the demonstrated outcomes or improved performances resulting from the goal?
19. How does the system encourage professional growth?

20. Does the system recognize the collective efforts of groups (i.e., buildings, departments)?

APTITUDE FOR ADEPT LEADERSHIP

Stakeholders expect their leaders to not only create a high-performance organization but also address daily, routine situations, handle crisis events, and solve controversial issues. Adept leaders chart a district's direction by incrementally and continuously moving it toward the horizon of excellence.

Leadership does make a difference, but adept leadership makes all *the difference.*

Leadership in the twenty-first century requires savvy and adept leaders who embrace the challenges of the future in a collaborative and problem-solving manner and one that relies on research, experimentation, and instinct. Leaders also recognize that there is no shortcut to high-performing schools, and that journey involves goals that are vertical and horizontal as well as immediate, short-range, and long-range.

Leaders also recognize that the push for excellence and buy-in is inclusive and broad-based. The twenty-first-century leader is both a technician and a communicator. Adept twenty-first-century leaders also recognize the power of transparency, communication, and engagement of community and school constituency groups to develop goals and to acquire and prioritize the associated resources to reach them.

Begin by thinking about your communication style. Is it personal? Does it often include the embedded themes of the organization? Ask yourself how the organization demonstrates that it values the staff. How effective is the communication process? Can the staff immediately demonstrate an understanding of the organization's goals and actions plans?

Consider the decision-making process by reflecting on the following.

1. Make a list of stakeholders that you engage in the decision-making process.
2. What specific actions have leaders taken to turn the vision into a daily reality?
3. How have leaders demonstrated their belief in continuous improvement?
4. Illustrate how leadership demonstrates its commitment to collaboration.
5. How does the leadership seek feedback from its employees?
6. Cite an example of how leadership has utilized employee feedback.

7. Explain how all members of the organization share responsibility in the attainment of district goals.
8. What does participation in the decision-making process look like?
9. How do leaders attain goal buy-in?
10. What specific decisions have leaders taken to make their vision a daily reality?
11. Through their decision-making process, how have leaders demonstrated their belief in continuous improvement?

Adept leaders also recognize the importance of the community and how the leader connects the school to the community. Leaders must reflect on the following.

1. Describe how the schools are perceived as integral to the community.
2. Does the community view the school or district as the hub of the community?
3. Does the school have outreach programs, and does it provide open access to its facilities?
4. How does the district or school partner with the community?
5. Does the district provide adult training, growth, or learning activities?
6. How does the school or district engage parents in their children's education?
7. How does the school or district provide opportunities to involve parents in the decision-making process?
8. How does the district obtain feedback and input from parents?
9. How does the school or district build community support?
10. Describe what measures or processes must be implemented to improve two-way communication.

Adept leaders truly recognize the unique opportunity to collaborate with staff in charting the future for the school, district, students, and community.

If leaders embrace the four essential elements, reflect, and begin to consider strategically how to implement solutions aligned to the school and district outcomes, high-performance outcomes and results are possible.

ESSENTIAL IDEAS

- Reflection assists leaders in reexamining the core components of a school or district and the ability of those organizations to execute its strategy to improve student performance.

- Reflection focuses on questions related to alignment, an attitude focused on achievement, accountability, and adept leadership.
- The failure to reflect and later strategize from these reflections will severely limit the continuous-improvement process and limit the drive toward improved performance.
- Reflection is a beginning point from which issues are identified and from which strategic solutions to those issues are formulated.

III

Reaching for Higher Performance

The next several chapters provide concrete suggestions to position one's school or district to improve performance. These chapters also recommend stages to move through the process of improvement as well as offering strategies for the integration of key elements for high-performing outcomes as well as providing three case studies that illustrate the journey toward excellence. Finally, this section concludes with a moral argument to improve school and district performance.

Chapter Six

Making Schools and Districts High Performing

Throughout the United States, many districts and schools, along with the public, believe that they are providing a very good if not excellent education to their student bodies. Unfortunately too many of these districts have equated excellence and possibly higher performance with the quality of its facilities, the "cutting edge" of its technology, their funding base, or other factors that researchers have consistently determined may not translate into exemplary or high-performing student outcomes.

Some schools also equate student-achievement growth resulting from a disproportionate percentage of higher socioeconomic demographics as an indicator of success rather than understanding success to be predicated on the quality, effectiveness, and efficiency in the delivery of the educational program to all students.

While exemplary facilities, the latest technology, and a strong funding base might provide some districts with a solid foundation on which to build successes, none of these factors individually or collectively can guarantee success. Our experience in working in districts throughout the United States and the Caribbean has shown us that well-intentioned, misaligned initiatives abound in affluent districts with ample resources as much as they do in struggling, low-income, and underperforming districts.

In 2012 and 2013 New Jersey's Camden School District, an inner-city school district, spent $27,400 per pupil, which is more than nine thousand dollars more than the state average, to educate approximately 11,700 students attending public schools. Advocates of increased public funding might be surprised to learn that even with this level of expenditure, "twenty-three of the district's twenty-six schools appeared on the state's list of the seventy lowest-performing schools." Paymon Rouhanifard, state-appointed superintendent, said, "we don't have a lack of resources here. We have an improper allocation of those resources."[1]

In 2006 Microsoft partnered with the School District of Philadelphia to build a School of the Future in which every student would have a laptop or, at the very least, access to a computer during the school day. After spending sixty-two million dollars to create a state-of-the-art building with cutting-edge technology, "the first set of state standardized test scores revealed that eleventh graders did no better than those at other comprehensive nonselective city high schools with about one-quarter of the students meeting reading-proficiency levels and only 7 percent of the student body reaching proficiency in math."[2]

As illustrated, the existence of programs and resources or infusions of funding alone isn't necessarily the solution to creating higher-performing schools. Also, required mandates, new evaluation systems, and other reform efforts are insufficient substitutes to effective alignment and execution in the efforts to meet the needs of all students. Adept leaders recognize the daily challenges of leadership but cannot be distracted by them. Leaders must continually focus the organization on its vision and high-performance outcomes.

As a school leader, by now you may recognize the importance of alignment, attitude, accountability, and having an aptitude for leadership. But the question remains, how do you ensure high performance for all students?

FOCUS THE ORGANIZATION!

In an interview with ABC news correspondent Rebecca Jarvis regarding the culture and leadership at Google, Jonathan Rosenberg and Eric Schmidt indicated that it is essential for an organization to focus on its mission and create a culture in which all employees have real buy-in to its direction.[3]

To move in the direction of higher performance, school boards and leaders must recognize that no commodity is as valuable as visionary leadership that is adept at executing the goals of the district and having employees who respond to it. It is visionary leadership that creates an environment of collective ownership so that all groups share direct responsibility regarding the implementation of initiatives. It is visionary leadership that provides the framework to connect the dots, to align all aspects of the organization for maximum performance.

At the same time, it is the leader's responsibility to ensure that the vision, the goals, and the strategies of the district represent outcomes that provide a foundation for higher performance. Becoming higher performing is the grunt work of administrators, teachers, parents, and students. This work requires savvy leadership to negotiate the myriad mandates, standards, and other requirements that often shift the focus of the organization or its vision.

From our experience, it is painfully evident that schools and districts do not recognize the connection between the four elements—alignment, attitude, accountability, and adept leadership—to higher performance. It is also evident that with the implementation of mandates and the layering of programs the direction toward higher performance is often confused. Unfortunately, we have also witnessed that most states require the existence of a strategic plan but fail to require that the efficiency of an organization play a role in planning for higher performance.

To assist leaders in focusing the organization, this book has integrated key components from such systems as the Baldrige Quality Model, Six Sigma, Accreditation for Growth, and others with our practical experiences and observations. Overall, these models provide a leadership and management framework that focuses an organization on its vision, mission, core values, and performance goals.

Schools and districts around the country—like the city of Pewaukee in Wisconsin, Maryland's Montgomery County Public Schools, Iredell-Statesville schools in North Carolina, and Jencks in Oklahoma, among others—have clearly demonstrated how to combine a quality model/framework with a laser focus on academics and organizational effectiveness that resulted in their ability to successfully implement their vision and mission along with reaching their goals. Regardless of the model utilized, we have found that a philosophy of continuous improvement throughout the organization is a necessary piece of the high-performance puzzle.

So if the answer is evident, then why is the reality of high-performing schools for all students so elusive? The answer lies in the narrow view of school improvement nurtured through the concept of mandates, the politicization of our educational system, a press that focuses on problems versus real solutions, and schools that focus on variables perceived to be insurmountable.

Again, from our experience, schools and districts must eliminate the distracting noise that keeps leaders from moving their districts to higher performance. Certainly it requires leaders with courage and the foresight to focus the district on its academic and performance priorities. It requires leaders who understand the nuances of the implementation process and have the foresight to utilize an improvement model that addresses all educational areas in an integrated manner necessary for higher performance.

We have dedicated our careers to creating high-performance schools and districts and know that without focus, a district will haphazardly hope to reach higher outcomes. With a model or framework that integrates the four elements of alignment, attitude, accountability, and adept leadership, we are confident that higher-performing schools can become a reality.

FOCUS ON BUY-IN!

Leaders face no task more difficult than building consensus and then executing the plan as designed.

To achieve buy-in, school boards and leaders must recognize that, while visionary leadership and results-based goals set the stage, having employees embrace the district vision and have them willingly execute it is essential to the plan's success. It is the people skills of the leader combined with visionary leadership that creates the collective buy-in required throughout the implementation process.

We also have mentioned that there are nuances in the implementation process of any plan that can make a difference between success and failure. The human factor is one such nuance. The human factor always begins with awareness and ends with awareness.

Data, while a part of creating awareness, is not the answer alone. When data paints a picture without considering the efforts of those who have contributed to the organization, the results can be demoralizing and devastating. Data analysis without considering the human factor can also result in a defensive reaction that builds a wall resistant to change. It is essential to have data touch the human fabric of an organization that appeals to a higher moral drive to improve performance for all children.

An adept leader understands the importance of creating the awareness in a manner that motivates the majority of the staff to see and desire a better outcome. The old top-down model has proven time and time again to not produce the sustained changes necessary to change the culture necessary to make a difference. Rather, the top-down model creates another barrier to change. If a culture embraces the change, the likelihood of sustainability increases.

We have found that true input and collaboration are the keys to successful buy-in. Try utilizing questions framed in a success format or outcome for a proven method to involve key stakeholder participation in changing the culture. Book studies, visitations to observe best practices, discussion groups, conference attendance, and the utilization of research can also increase stakeholder participation.

DEVELOP A POSITIVE ATMOSPHERE BUILT AROUND ACHIEVEMENT!

To paraphrase Charles Darwin, a species survives by how it responds to change.[4] John Kotter, of Harvard Business School, illustrates the challenges of organizational change and directional adjustment in *Our Iceberg Is Melting*.[5] In the allegorical work, challenges faced by a flock of penguins on an iceberg require an in-depth examination of historical practices and an adjustment in both the decision-making paradigm and other beliefs.

The challenges confronting schools and districts require similar reflection and analysis. Low student achievement, achievement gaps, and poor skill acquisition continue to plague too many schools despite increased scrutiny and legislative pressure for reform and improvement. Solutions for improvement often include "silver bullet "recommendations, but our country's ability to compete globally is tangential to our ability to change the internal culture of a school or district. In the context of reform or improvement, oppositional statements such as "This too shall pass" are all too common.

Sir Edward Tylor described culture as "that complex whole which includes knowledge, belief, art, morals, law custom, and other capabilities and habits acquired by man as a member of society."[6] Simply, it is "the way we do things around here."

Culture is dependent on the core values of an organization. Unfortunately, many districts have never developed or have never been required to develop organizational core values. If, indeed, they were developed, questions would arise regarding how effectively they are reflected in the organization, since many districts have not collectively defined the meaning of *core values*. Without a collective process that develops an understanding of the organization's core values, they are just words, open to interpretation by each individual of the organization.

In his memoir, *Duty*, Robert Gates, former US Secretary of Defense, lamented "a challenge of culture of multiple competing interests at the Department of Defense but encouraged communication, transparency, candor, and teamwork during his transition to the position as Secretary of Defense."[7] Not unlike large bureaucratic governmental organizations, schools and districts have a series of internal structures—policies, programs, and entire departments—that support the status quo along with the institutional dynamics and traditional mores of staff that are resistant to change.

Whether assuming the leadership of a failing school or of a district that is perceived to be successful, the challenge of culture change is equally daunting. Regardless of the school's status, an educational leader must create a sense of urgency for change through the utilization and examination of concrete data.

Values, beliefs, program effectiveness, and alignment require review in an objective manner. The dialogue around such an analysis generally infuses the organization with a sense of inclusiveness and empowerment. Any organizational disjointedness and dysfunction should be exposed by such a review. Further examination and candor may highlight deficiencies in organizational capacity and related resources required to attain the desired outcomes.

Prior to designing a model for change, school leaders should consider three distinct areas: obstacles, data, and process. When obstacles to change are identified and anticipated, practical solutions to overcome them must be identified in advance to prevent the improvement effort from being sidetracked.

Consider the type of data required for an effective analysis of the school or district's current state, how the data link with the curriculum and methodology, and how the data are acquired, stored, disseminated, and reviewed. It is essential that any data review be inclusive and discussed in a variety of forums. These discussions will assist in building the urgency for change and the subsequent consensus required to move forward.

Creating a high-performing school for all students is indeed the heavy lifting of school leadership. Failing schools perceive the leap as impossible, while successful schools are often comfortable with the status quo. Both the failing school and successful school face unique challenges in moving toward higher performance.

Professional staff and even parents might express concern or even mount opposition to such a direction for a variety of reasons, many of which are personal and experiential. To diffuse such concerns, an honest, collaborative, and open dialogue focusing on the following questions may provide a recentered perspective.

1. What do you want for your children/students?
2. To fulfill your child's/student's potential, what do you believe needs to be done?
3. What do you believe that your children/students need to know to be successful?
4. How do you think that we compare as a school locally, regionally, nationally, and internationally?
5. What needs to be adjusted?

Obviously for a school leader to facilitate such a conversation, advance preparation involving performance data, statistical trends, and knowledge of best practices that produce optimum outcomes is required. The challenge for a school leader is to facilitate the conversation in a manner that provides the detail, data, and pedagogical understanding in a collaborative manner that allows for an objective, logical, and consensus-based recommendation.

"Much like in the field of medicine, educational decisions should be based on factual evidence, research, and data rather than opinion."[8] By establishing an evidence-based ground rule, discussions focus on effective practices and research-based instruction.

BUILD A CULTURE OF ACCOUNTABILITY!

For the most part, every school or district has participated to some degree in the development of goals, but "student achievement in the US still lags behind schools in most developed countries." Researchers at the renowned Brookings Institution in a recent publication, *Endangering Prosperity*, indicate that even neighboring "Canada ranks in the top third of student achievement in mathematics proficiency while the performance in the United States is similar to those in countries such as Latvia and Lithuania."[9] In fact, these researchers negate the impact on achievement by the frequently cited issues of demographics, economics, and funding.

With so much effort expended on improvement, why are too many schools and districts still lagging behind? The answer lies with the inability of the leader to execute the strategies necessary to achieve its goals. "It is the missing link between aspirations and results."[10]

Disconnection leads to nuances involving alignment of goals to achievement outcomes, the inclusiveness of the process, the quality of the data, the depth of analysis, understanding and respecting the importance of the human factor in school improvement, and the integration of those goals into the fabric of the school or district, along with the associated issues of implementation, accountability, and resource allocation.

Too often faculty members lament the administration's obsession with minutiae and the lack of commitment to attain substantive results. Additionally, political agendas and other favorite projects too often result in the board of education relegating the school or district's primary mission to the back burner and selecting school-leadership personnel who will maintain the status quo. All of these issues then lend themselves to the tendency of implementing one new program after another and not focusing on those elements that are in place and need to be improved.

From the outset, the success of goal development and the integration of the goals are directly related to the inclusiveness of the process and eventually how staff members are empowered to implement those goals. Clearly the school leader must facilitate the process by framing a model for interactions of key constituency groups such as the board, teachers, and parents.

Coordination, oversight, and, most importantly, action leadership is critical at this level. While a successful development process has a clear relationship to inclusiveness and empowerment, successful implementation is directly related to an environment of accountability and resources. A senior leader must take an active role in order to provide the support, necessary resources, and motivation needed to realize the intended goals.

The entire plan must cycle all the components back to the school and district's vision, mission, core values, achievement, and outcomes. Successful outcomes occur when the leader translates these components into action so the school or district and the community live the plan each and every day.

Also critical to the development process is the delineation of clear outcomes from the outset, along with defining indicators of success to measure those outcomes. State standardized measures vary widely regarding the level of skill acquisition, while the "Program for International Student Assessment (PISA) might provide a more realistic frame of reference for national and international comparisons."[11] Understanding the content of such an assessment and knowing the student's strengths and weaknesses are invaluable in the planning process.

Additionally, locally developed authentic assessments provide invaluable information particularly when linked to planned systemic benchmark assessments. Nonetheless, a comprehensive district-wide assessment involving dialogue focused on strengths and weaknesses in the context of student achievement is essential to providing a boots-on-the-ground perspective. In conducting the school- or district-wide assessment, it is significant that past accomplishments and achievement be recognized as part of what we call an *appreciative review*.

Celebrating the past and beginning with positive feedback honors those who have genuinely attempted to improve the lives of students even though the results may have been somewhat suspect or statistically insignificant. Well-intentioned programs, policies, procedures, and curriculum initiatives are exposed through an in-depth analysis of data and learning versus unsubstantiated opinion. Data such as grading patterns, failure rates, retention, and achievement gaps in the context of race, ethnicity, and special populations can assist in framing goals. The entire process crystallizes the axiom that good inputs equal good outputs.

Even more important is determining the composition of school-improvement teams. For an effectively aligned plan to actually come to fruition, school leaders must select an improvement team based on technical expertise and one devoid of personal agendas. Teams often utilize a cross section of school-based curriculum experts balanced with critical support staff with the option of utilizing district supervisory expertise on an ad hoc basis. To assure alignment and compliance with improvement designs, a review process at the district level provides a rudimentary system of checks and balances.

Since there is no activity that is more high stakes than charting the direction of a district, the review process should consider the following critical questions.

1. Do the goals align with school and district values? Is the goal-development process inclusive?

2. What assessments/data are utilized in establishing the goals? Does the utilized data thoroughly provide insight into student performance? How are the goals measured?
3. Are the goals integrated into the fabric of the district?
4. Do the goals incorporate classroom-tested research?
5. Are the goals realistic or incremental based on the district's current capacity?
6. What is the role of the district's leadership in goal development? Do all groups assume an equitable share of responsibility in the execution of the goals?

It is without question that schools and districts have a moral responsibility to improve, change, and create a dynamic environment for instruction and learning. To become an effective school or district, programs and resources may require prioritization and reallocation based on their effectiveness and impact on student-achievement outcomes. In doing so, a school leader must be cognizant of the impact of such analysis.

Remember that the change and improvement process is personal. While a moral imperative clearly exists to change a culture of underachievement so that it ultimately increases student potential, never discount how the actual change might impact the careers effected by it. Without buy-in, the best-laid plan often fails.

Once consensus is attained, the leader and team develop aligned action plans to reach high-performance outcomes. The plan is essentially an outline of various steps to reach the defined goals in a collaborative and participatory manner. In the plan, it is critical to incorporate the previously discussed components involving alignment, attitude, accountability, and aptitude for leadership.

PLANNING

What differentiates this process from strategic planning is that it is dynamic, focused on student outcomes, and designed for immediate results with action steps directly correlated to student growth, achievement, and organizational excellence. The plan is referenced daily, weekly, monitored regularly, and is fluid, based on key indicators of success. All decisions are prioritized as they relate to their impact on achievement.

Upon reviewing the master plan for improvement we had written for a school we were working with, Jerry Anderson—former principal of Brazosport High School in Freeport, Texas, who has been recognized for improving student achievement—told us that if we managed to accomplish what we intended, we would make it a top-tier school in the United States. He was right; it took seven years to get there, but we never became complacent.

Likewise, over the same period in another school district we worked with, student proficiency increased every year, participation in advanced placement increased by over 200 percent, and the district was able to significantly close the achievement gap for all student groups. As a result, that district was awarded the top gold medal ranking in multiple years by *Expansion Management Magazine*, which evaluates the education quotient (EQ) of districts or businesses looking to relocate or expand into desirable locations.

Unlike many other educational ratings that equate excellence to the level of public funding received, EQ focuses primarily on results. One of the key indices evaluated is how well students learn and how many stay in school to graduate.

Creating a plan and environment to improve district performance and to create a highly effective school and district is highly challenging for even the most gifted of school leaders. Assuring alignment of a plan to all components of the district requires leadership that recognizes the importance of an inclusive approach that is empowering and facilitating.

A shift to world-class outcomes requires improvement teams with the technical expertise to articulate a visionary plan. While this all sounds quite daunting, we believe that the experiences and insights provided in this book will assist you in creating the same learning environments that we were able to build as superintendents. It is about leadership, vision, and execution.

Remember, as a school or district you are either improving, maintaining the status quo, or falling behind. Now get started by

- aligning the organization for efficiency and effectiveness
- developing a climate in which attitude equals altitude
- building a culture of collaborative accountability
- developing an aptitude for adept leadership.

Remember, as a school leader you have to eliminate the weeds and look beyond the trees to the horizon, but always know that as you move forward, so does the horizon.

ESSENTIAL IDEAS

- All schools can improve and reach higher levels of performance regardless of the obstacles and challenges.
- Performance and quality are not exclusively functions of money or facilities.

- Underperformance is often related to well-intentioned, misaligned initiatives existing in both affluent and low-income schools.
- School boards and leaders must recognize that no commodity is as valuable as a leader adept at executing the goals of the school or district.
- Leaders *focus the organization* through visionary, savvy leadership that utilizes a framework as a guideline.
- Leaders understand the nuances of the implementation process.
- Leaders *focus on buy-in* through consensus building, creating awareness that touches the human fabric of the organization.
- *Develop a positive atmosphere* built around achievement by understanding the power of the organizational culture and how to change it.
- *Build a culture of accountability* that is embraced by all stakeholders.
- Successful outcomes occur when leaders are able to translate goals into action.
- The change and improvement process is personal, dynamic, and designed for immediate results.

Chapter Seven

Planning for Success

We believe that school leaders have the internal capacity to improve student achievement but often get overwhelmed as to where to begin or have attempted approaches that are very formulaic in nature and have not produced the anticipated desired results.

In planning for successful change, it is critical to obtain feedback and listen to all stakeholders, gather information, assess, and examine proven strategies that when tailored will produce the targeted results.

Success for this process is found within the nuances of how these interactions take place and whether stakeholders see that the suggested input and feedback is acted upon. We recognize that there is more than one approach to reach excellence but also recognize that there are key building blocks that must be incorporated into any system of improvement. We believe that the foundation for success should be built in five stages—(1) understanding the concepts and building blocks for success, (2) identifying, exploring, and assessing the foundation of success, (3) the development of focused school or district improvement plans, (4) the implementation, and (5) monitoring, follow-up, and support.

STAGE 1: UNDERSTANDING THE CONCEPTS AND BUILDING BLOCKS FOR SUCCESS

Nonformulaic/Customized Plan

Every school and district is unique unto itself. Preconceived perceptions of the situational dynamics of an organization often lead to internal tension and a lack of trust. It is essential that school leaders listen and sort out the issues and areas of concern as to what are real and what are unfounded. Too often there are internal, illogical reasons for maintaining programs, policies, procedures, and initiatives that obstruct progress.

Breaking down the barriers to progress requires listening, information gathering, and data gathering to build a compelling reason to change the current practices. At the same time it is critical in the school-improvement process to recognize past and present traditions as well as strengths of the school or district. For the most part, all schools and districts have implemented initiatives that are successful, and it is essential to maintain those initiatives contributing to high-performance outcomes.

Given that some initiatives and approaches have worked while others probably need to be abandoned or modified, a customized improvement plan building on the school or district's strengths in a collaborative manner is essential.

Framework for High Performance

Upon embarking on the path to high performance, school leaders need to consider how to integrate a philosophy into the endeavor that is universally embraced and modeled. As previously indicated, the incorporation of principles such as the *correlates of effective schools*[1] or a similar framework provide effective guidelines in decision making and change the focus of the organization.

Frameworks often provide guidelines in the development of goals and measurable actions plans that guide the delivery of instruction. The system of accountability measuring both student and staff performance will also be tied directly to the framework.

The sustainability of this framework is also tied directly to its effectiveness and the buy-in from staff in its creation. In a collaborative process in building the framework, the conversation should focus on achievement data, obstacles, resource allocation, and other relevant variables impacting school improvement that are specific to a school or district. Personal ownership is developed through this collaborative dialogue. Discussion topics often involve the following questions.

- What are the components to a framework of success?
- Does the framework incorporate school district data and an analysis of effective practices?
- Will the plan provide a foundation for improving school achievement?
- Does the plan really measure student progress?

Essential Elements

We have previously discussed the importance of understanding the four essential elements, which, if implemented in an integrated manner, will maximize instructional outcomes for students. Through the application of these key elements, we are confident that student achievement will grow dramatically. While not a dramatically new concept, the difference is how these elements are integrated into the fabric of the district. Often, each is viewed separately and rarely do leaders consider their interrelationship.

Fundamental to becoming a high-performing school or district is the ability to:

- align the school and district's mission, vision, and goals
- create an atmosphere of continuous improvement
- implement a collective accountability system based on how a rigorous curriculum is delivered
- and foster adept leadership in the implementation of a school-improvement model.

The analysis of each of these elements and the interrelationship of each in relation to student achievement in a school or district will reveal avenues and opportunities for improvement.

STAGE 2: IDENTIFYING, EXPLORING, AND ASSESSING THE FOUNDATION OF SUCCESS

Organizational Reflection and Assessment

Leaders need to probe an organization to honestly examine and evaluate what is working and to identify areas for improvement. By utilizing a variety of instruments and techniques that incorporate the key elements of alignment, atmosphere, accountability, and adept leadership, a portrait of a school or district's effectiveness emerges. Some of these tools include:

- self-reflection
- cross-checking
- organizational assessments

In chapter 5, we encouraged leaders to reflect upon the effectiveness of the organization through a lens embodying the components of the four elements. In addition, we also believe that an analysis of the strength or prevalence of each essential element as perceived by various constituency groups within the organization provides revealing data as to a school or district's effectiveness. This process known as *cross-checking* highlights both strengths and disconnections between stakeholder groups.

Too often, in an attempt to improve student achievement, schools and districts layer program on top of program. This layering effect unintentionally results in disconnectedness—and a lack of instructional connectivity especially.

The school systems cross-check detailed in appendix B allows you to examine the interconnection of school and district processes and programs by cross-checking embedded performance elements in key organizational areas. The process seeks clear demonstrations of those elements and makes immediate, short-, and long-range recommendations that will result in a more effective school or district.

Part of the school systems cross-check process is an organization assessment that includes a document review examining and analyzing the impact of school and district policies on student achievement and school or district effectiveness. Areas of review include but are not limited to:

- strategic plans
- school and district goals
- human-resources recruitment and hiring practices
- curriculum and programming
- instructional practices and methodology
- systems of assessment and achievement data
- observation/supervision and evaluation practices
- professional development
- financial planning/budgets/priorities and allocations
- communications plans
- and board policies.

Summarizing disconnections includes an evaluation of the findings from the cross-check and organizational assessment to identify priorities for improvement and flaws in the planning process.

Essential in the organizational reflection and assessment process is the communication of the findings to all stakeholders and participating groups.

Communication of the findings assists with clarifying conclusions and recommendations, builds support in the developing consensus regarding priorities and goals, and increases transparency, which further promotes inclusion and collaboration for the overall process.

STAGE 3: DEVELOPMENT OF FOCUSED SCHOOL OR DISTRICT IMPROVEMENT PLANS

Prior to the development of an improvement plan, it is worthwhile to informally learn how a school or district perceives its performance. The responses are often eye-opening and might include language like, "We are excellent," "We do the best we can," "What can they honestly expect," and so on.

The data often reveal a different scenario, but, more importantly, it is important to listen to their dreams. What type of school do they want to be? Not only are these essential questions to ask staff, but parents, too, should be asked. What are their aspirations? Do they believe those aspirations are possible? And the bigger question, is, "How do *we* get there together?" From experience, we know that we get there together with a focused improvement design.

Focused Design

A focused design squarely targets improving student achievement and increasing overall school and district performance. The design reflects the utilization of data in the development of priorities and goals but also recognizes the importance of collaboration and stakeholder input.

Through this collaborative process, all members of the organization endorse outcomes that drive the organization toward higher performance. Achievement and performance-related decisions are made in the context of the design. This type of design also recognizes the importance of shared responsibility in goal attainment.

Critical components in a focused design to improve achievement and to improve performance include:

- defining processes in the analysis of data, establishing priorities, developing goals, identifying outcomes, allocating resources, and monitoring growth
- defining the decision-making process
- action plans that address identified achievement and performance issues
- balanced and shared responsibility for goal attainment
- an allocation of resources that reflects the organization's commitment to higher performance for all students
- time lines aligned with the recommended goals
- transparent accountability for monitoring plan completion
- professional development based on organizational priorities, goals, and designated outcomes
- and implementation strategies.

STAGE 4: IMPLEMENTATION

Proven Practices

As part of the implementation stage, it is critical to include strategies that are consistent with the four essential elements. Without giving special attention to incorporating best practices for proper alignment, attitude, accountability systems, and adept leadership, the desired higher performance will not be attained. It is important that leaders and facilitators utilize proven best practices that align with the targeted outcomes.

For a variety of reasons, in response to the complex issue of student achievement and higher school performance, schools and districts implement strategies and practices that are in vogue, rather than relying on proven and research-driven practices. Simply endorsing an unproven program will result in frustration within the system, layering of programs, and eroding confidence in the plan.

Components that a leader should consider when implementing an improvement plan in a strategic manner should include:

- strategically allocated resources
- maintaining transparency at all times
- recognizing the importance of communication
- maintaining accountability and shared responsibility at all levels
- recognizing the importance of growing human capacity
- and incorporating an adept-leadership training program.

STAGE 5: MONITORING, FOLLOW-UP, AND SUPPORT

Monitoring and Encouraging Growth

An effective monitoring system with benchmarks and indicators of success enables the school or district to monitor growth and immediately adjust to variables based on data. Both individual- and collective-accountability systems monitor the consistency of implementation and encourage growth in the organization. It is key to consider the type of observation and evaluation systems and the manner in which an organization links curriculum, instruction, and assessment to them.

Getting everyone on the same page is critical, but keeping them on that page and turning the page as the organization moves forward is equally important. Often the most overlooked and underfunded component in the organization is its professional-development program. Investing in staff development not only builds capacity but also builds enthusiasm and ownership.

Effective components in the monitoring, follow-up, and support process include:

- supervising and evaluating for high-performance outcomes
- professional-development planning
- and a communication plan.

ESSENTIAL IDEAS

- The foundation to planning for success includes understanding the concepts and building blocks for success.
- Leaders must identify, explore, and assess each school or district's foundation for success.
- Successful planning for higher-performance outcomes requires the development of school- and district-improvement plans that are measurable and focused on achievement.
- Implementation for success must involve proven practices.
- Sustainable performance requires measurement, monitoring, and professional growth.

Chapter Eight

Strategies for Success

ALIGNMENT

The Conductor

An administrator's role in many ways is like that of a conductor of an orchestra or chorus. Rather than direct the performers involved, an administrator directs a school, a department, or an entire school district. For sure, it is full of voices and sounds and expectations; in the same way that a conductor coordinates the work of performers to result in a coherent music experience that moves the audience, so the administrator creates a type of harmony.

The conductor is crucial to the performance of the orchestra or chorus. A conductor's primary responsibilities and skills include researching pieces of work and interpreting the composer's vision for the performers and the audience. As the performance begins, the conductor must be adept at the execution of the music in order to produce a high-quality experience. Most importantly, an effective conductor is adept at bringing together in a unified sound a diverse group of performers who each has their own style.

Upon appointment to an educational-leadership position, every administrator realizes that these skills of coordination, facilitation, and execution are essential in fulfilling the responsibilities of the position. Sitting in the chair of educational leadership immediately provides the individual an entirely different perspective of what is necessary to be effective. Rather than completing one component of a task, an administrator needs to coordinate the work of many. In short order, you learn that the buck doesn't stop at your desk. If an administrator is unable to bring various constituencies together, the desired goals of a school or district will have little chance to succeed.

A superintendent colleague once explained that an awareness regarding the scope of the position hit home after he attended his first board meeting. The agenda had been developed based on the business of the month. While senior leadership worked on the agenda, the superintendent had felt that he'd need to be the go-to person if the board had questions. He'd prepared and prepared to ensure that he would have the answers to any question the board might ask, which would clearly distinguish him as leader of the organization.

The day of the board meeting, the public in attendance and those who watched its broadcast on the local cable station would certainly have been in awe of his competence; the superintendent was prepared to answer big-picture questions as well as speak knowledgeably on even the smallest details—everything about student lunches to Johnny's comprehension problems.

By the meeting's conclusion, however, his confidence had been somewhat shaken. Not one question had been directed to him. Was it the board's version of a honeymoon period, or did the board not have confidence in his leadership skills? He wondered if they'd hired the right person.

At the meeting, when questions had been raised about the district's buildings, they'd been directed to the director of facilities. Questions about the high school had been directed to the assistant superintendent. "It appeared on the surface," the superintendent confided to me, "that my position was reduced to reading the agenda, having board members respond to it by directing questions to cabinet members."

Again, he wondered, had the board lost confidence in him already, or was this the culture of the district? He later expressed these same concerns to the board president, pointing out that the buck stopped with the superintendent. The president responded that board simply wanted the person closest to the issue to address any questions; in other words, it was the leader's responsibility to orchestrate the work of the more than two thousand employees.

In short order and over time, the superintendent learned just how important this orchestration was as well as how difficult it was to bring together diverse groups to achieve a successful result. Planning, perseverance, and listening to feedback from various constituencies, like the work of a conductor, would result in a high-quality performance or, in educational terms, the achievement of the desired result.

As Bossidy and Charan have discovered, "Execution is not just tactics—it is discipline and system. It has to be built into a company's strategy, its goals and culture." And for it to be successful, "the leader must be deeply engaged in it."[1]

Time and time again as a consultant, we have clearly observed a lack of support and direction for these plans and their associated goals. There is compelling evidence of the lack of alignment to these plans or, worse, evidence of poor planning in the development of them altogether.

Even when a school or district has a vision and mission statement, espousing organizational values, questions often arise regarding the alignment of those values with outcomes, the integration of those values, and the internalization of them. The organizational challenge is for members of the organization to live those values every day. This section provides you with the strategies and frameworks in which to coordinate, facilitate, and align the school or district's vision, mission, values, plans, and goals to its targeted high-performance outcomes.

To assist in building a strong foundation that aligns the organization, the following strategies and resources are recommended.

1. Consider adopting an instructional model that focuses on continuous improvement, such as the Correlates of Effective Schools.
2. Develop a decision-making framework that links all decisions to input, best practices, and student achievement.
3. Develop an inclusionary problem-solving model.
4. Develop a set of organizational values that address all aspects of the organization and is aligned to the school or district's vision (see examples in appendix A, activity #1).
5. As part of the strategic plan, develop yearly goals that are defined and measurable.
6. Research and explore the Baldrige Education Criteria for Performance Excellence, continuous-improvement models, Sigma Six certification, and ISO 9001.
7. Create and articulate a process of internal assessment and data analysis.
8. Formulate a departmental-improvement advisory council to parallel the Effective Schools methodology to align the operational side of the district with the instructional vision, mission, and values.
9. Consider the Ritz-Carlton Daily Line-Up to reinforce and communicate values, goals, and beliefs.
10. Examine appendix A, activities #1 and 2.

ATTITUDE AND ATMOSPHERE

Me, We, Us

Collaboration, empowerment, engagement, and *satisfaction* are words commonly heard in organizations to demonstrate to constituents that the organization really cares and wants to involve everyone. Research provides article after article pointing to the necessity of creating a culture to support these concepts, along with numerous examples of how to make a collaborative culture a reality. However, it is much more difficult to create this culture than one might expect.

Southwest Airlines, the Ritz-Carlton Hotel Company, LinkedIn Corporation, Google Inc., and Nike, Inc. are some organizations that have been recognized for high employee satisfaction. These companies all follow and practice the mantra of putting people first. They know that so doing will more effectively meet their goals and improve the bottom line. The challenge with a school and district is to create a collaborative culture operating with an embedded philosophy of continuous improvement and one that places children first.

While more and more school districts are utilizing employee-satisfaction surveys, the utilization of the data from the survey often doesn't appear to produce the desired results. When working as consultants with teachers and administrators around the country, we clearly observed that greater attention is necessary in this area, because there is an obvious disconnect between initiatives, programs, mission, vision, and outcomes of the school or district.

Personally, I hear time and again assurances when completing a training session—in my case, on supervision and evaluation—that "This too shall pass." Teachers and staff members have expressed in a variety of ways that they have no ownership of the program. For the most part, there is a great sense that they are isolated and removed from the decision-making process or from input regarding what makes a difference.

When interviewing for a position, it is rare that all issues and problems are discussed. So it was only upon assuming the position of superintendent in a large, diverse school district, within days of meeting the staff, that it became clear to me that employee morale was in need of improvement. Relationships between the school board and the teachers had been strained for many years. Many teachers were unhappy with the top-down management style of the district office and the principals. Not unique to this district, the teachers felt underappreciated.

What was somewhat unique is that some board members in so many words made it clear that they felt satisfaction, collaboration, and so on—soft indicators of success were not important; after all, they were being paid to do a job.

A crack-the-whip mentality predominated. Nothing else was necessary.

A board member actually told me to make it difficult for the teaching staff to get access to me. This member wanted me to "show them that you are the boss" and they needed to "buckle down, shut up, and do the job that they were hired to do." In other words, their input and knowledge was unwelcome.

Also, in working with the administrative team, while many spoke of collaboration and input, the overall management style of these middle managers did not represent it. It was a command-and-control style dictated by those running the district, the school board.

Obviously, there was a lot of work to be done if we were to become collaborative. So, we undertook a campaign to begin to change the culture of the district and truly engage and collaborate with our staff.

An employee-satisfaction survey was one of the first steps in our journey. While staff feedback focused on the great job they were doing, cited opportunities for improvement included appreciation for employee efforts, better communication, fairness in applying school and district rules, and administrative trust. Not surprisingly, the finger-pointing was in one direction—away from themselves; there was very little self-introspection. But it was clearly too early to expect much different.

The administrative team began by utilizing a series of books to begin the dialogue at the leadership level. The following books offered insight into the importance of listening to employees and how it can be transformational to the organization. Some of the strategies that would eventually be implemented were gleaned by leaders in this area and were easily converted into the educational arena. The discussion books included:

- *Good to Great: Why Some Companies Make the Leap . . . and Others Don't*, by Jim Collins (2001)
- *The New Gold Standard: 5 Leadership Principles for Creating a Legendary Customer Experience Courtesy of the Ritz-Carlton Hotel Company*, by Joseph A. Michelli (2008)
- *The 3 Keys to Empowerment: Release the Power within People for Astonishing Results*, 2nd ed., by Kenneth H. Blanchard, John P. Carlos, and W. Alan Randolph (2001)
- *The 8th Habit: From Effectiveness to Greatness*, by Stephen R. Covey (2005).

We learned that the staff, who for the most part loved their jobs, felt underappreciated. They sought to be more involved and included in the decision-making process. It was clear that we had a dedicated and talented staff. The question became how to unleash their potential to create a more effective organization.

Now that we had the feedback, we started an initiative we called People Services. We formed teams to address various aspects of employee engagement, decision making, and empowerment. We began a training program for our leadership team to identify and begin fostering the necessary culture and to celebrate our employees. The work included developing our foundation, *core values, mission, and vision, which served as a basis for what we called a "people-centered organization," one that places the students first.*

We wanted to build relationships, communicate consistently, and value the knowledge and skills of those in the organization. Doing so was one of the most satisfying experiences during my tenure, because it changed the culture of the organization. A satisfied staff that worked in tandem with its administration enabled the school and district to maximize its efforts in the delivery of instructional services for all students. When self-reflection (me), intersects with collaboration (we) and implementation (us), great things can occur.

In conjunction to these initiatives discussed, it is recommended that the collaborative processes are included in key district structures. Other areas for consideration include

- a strategic hiring process that is inclusive
- induction, mentoring, and coaching models
- a customer-satisfaction program
- employee-satisfaction assessments
- tiered and targeted professional development
- a program for the development of teacher-leaders (a career-ladder or master-teacher program; see appendix D)
- and the specific suggestions in appendix A, activity #3.

Remember that while including attitudinal valued characteristics in the alignment of the aforementioned structures is critical, nothing is more powerful than modeling, guidance, and support.

ACCOUNTABILITY

Just Good Enough?

Educators have lived in an era of accountability for years. Required national, state, and local testing, revised teacher- and administrator-evaluation frameworks, budgetary restrictions, and mandates by the basketful have been part of the educational landscape now for many years. Have these external pressures improved educational performance as intended? Hearing the ongoing rhetoric from legislators, the questions from the press, and local community feedback, it would appear that they have not.

With such external pressure from a variety of forces, the obvious question is, Why not? We speculate that the answer is one of design. For an accountability system to truly function as designed, it must be collaboratively developed, designed around the delivery of curriculum and student outcomes.

Every member of the organization must have ownership of its outcomes; for when externally imposed systems of accountability are introduced without input from staff to modify and customize them, the system will not meet its desired results.

My time spent in the central office and as superintendent brought home to me the need for accountability in educational institutions. And this belief was only strengthened when I spent time in myriad districts around the country.

Over the years, I have met thousands of dedicated and hardworking educators who have truly wanted to improve their schools. They are good people but still struggle with the negative perception of education today that plays out in the press.

Through no fault of their own, too many schools and districts have failed to align. Some of these educators may also believe that their work is excellent but work in isolation. Others may rate the school or district as excellent, but they often come to this conclusion utilizing soft criteria, insufficiently focused on student performance or organizational outcome.

I have seen a number of wake-up calls demonstrating to educators a need to design and implement a realistic system that would guarantee better results.

At a public meeting, a school board member took issue in no uncertain terms with a review of the district's test scores. The superintendent had been painting a picture of a highly performing school district. A majority of our students were scoring in the proficient range. So the board member's observation was something of a curve ball.

This board member challenged the leadership's response to those students who were not proficient and angrily pointed out that tax dollars were not delivering intended results: the district's support failed to aid all *students. The board member expressed consternation that the district was satisfied with the results of high-performing students while failing to do enough for those who were not proficient.* The board member was correct.

The district had been basking in the recognition of a high school that had been awarded Blue Ribbon status by the Department of Education. In addition, the district had regularly produced a significant number of merit scholars. A very high percentage of the student body was going on to college, and the school's extracurricular programs had been achieving success "year in and year out," as they put it. Overall, the district leadership was pleased with the results.

Even so, the board president was able to point out inconsistent test scores, which showed significant increases in proficiency one year and decreases the next. Again, the board member was correct.

The district had been coasting on its reputation as a good school district. Overall, the feeling permeated that they were a great—even exemplary!—

district. And yet clearly there was work to do. The district, like many districts, did not have a well-articulated plan with built-in systems of accountability or a culture that support improved learning for all of its students. In reality, this district was merely good enough.

In addition to needing to develop a culture of continuous improvement, the district's need to understand its role in serving its constituents was illuminated by a parent complaint.

When attempting to return a lost book to the high school, the parent had been bounced from one person to another—treated with indifference and made to feel like an inconvenience. While this incident might seem innocuous, the parent's words resonated loud and clear: "If your organization was a business selling products, I would never return again; but I have no choice. You are the only realistic place for my child to get an education for my tax dollars."

The parent was correct. *Somehow the district had evolved into an insensitive and unwelcoming organization. It was clearly not grounded in the premise that its mission was to serve all students and its community.*

The board member's and the parent's complaints made it clear to me that our organization had to become more accountable. We needed to overhaul our belief system and mission to define the real meaning of student achievement. So, certain questions remained: How does a district develop a sense that accountability is obligatory? How do we provide better customer service rather than scramble only to meet the needs of the adults in an organization at the expense of our customers and children?

Over the years, we began to change this culture of complacency and poor customer service. It took time to move our staff in this direction. But by utilizing a continuous-improvement model that addressed both the academic side and operational side of the organization, we slowly turned the corner. Our strategy was to focus on the entire system, not just a segment of it.

We adopted a number of strategies that made the difference. Districts hoping to make similar changes should consider the following steps toward improvement.

Select an improvement framework that acts as a guideline for the district.

- Some options might include Effective Schools, the American Society for Quality, and the Baldrige Education Criteria; but whichever framework is chosen, customize the approach to make the initiative unique to the district.
- Most educators prefer an internally developed program for improvement versus one that is formulaic—or worse, one that is externally imposed.

Develop a data-assessment literacy plan.

- Have staff members understand the power of data, how it can be utilized, and where it can be found.
- Implement a comprehensive results–based building-goal process that includes collecting and organizing data, analyzing data, designing an action plan, and implementing the action plan.

Consider the following suggestions for building goal action-plan development.

- Review the results and data in relation to the proposed goal.
- Analyze the data: drill down to determine the probable cause for the issue or deficiency.
- Brainstorm improvement strategies.
- Prioritize solutions.
- Determine and quantify measurement indicators.
- Allocate resources commensurate with the complexity of the goal.
- Implement the action plan.
- Continually review progress toward goals, and adjust accordingly.

Develop an administrative and department action plan.

- Review the results and data or the current status related to identified goal areas.
- What strengths and weaknesses are revealed from a review of available data?
- What are the likely significant causes that produced the need for improvement?
- What are the final improvement opportunities and solutions?
- What is the purpose of the plan?
- Develop an action plan that requires regular updates.
- Make sure the action plan specifically delineates steps for each target.
- Delineate substeps as necessary.
- In each step, address accountability—responsibilities, measurement.
- For additional guidance, see appendix A, activity sheets #4 and 5.

ADEPT LEADERSHIP

Years ago, a professor in my graduate administrative program succinctly defined an administrator's responsibilities: "As a leader," he advised, "your main responsibility is to remove roadblocks so that teachers can teach and students can learn."

This former professor, once a successful superintendent, was viewed as an excellent leader, was highly respected, seemed to always get the job done, and handled difficult decisions with a flair. But this simple and succinct job description—"removing the roadblocks"—was always at the core of his work. At the same time, he recognized the importance of being an instructional leader, a coach, a cheerleader, and an advocate.

When I worked as a superintendent, I introduced this concept to teachers and staff. At times, the concept was taken out of context and applied to all types of decisions rather than the most important decisions related to student achievement.

Our administrative team strove to put the roadblock philosophy at the center of our work to reach the goal of educating all students. It looked different in different situations, but it was critical in moving our organization toward excellence.

The removal of roadblocks in itself finds its roots in servant leadership—a term coined by Robert Greenleaf and first published in 1970. "The servant leader is servant first," Greenleaf wrote. "It begins with the natural feeling that one wants to serve, to serve first. Then conscious choice brings one to aspire, to lead. That person is sharply different from one who is leader first, perhaps because of the need to assuage an unusual power drive or to acquire material possession."[2]

Administrative graduate courses are filled with academic distinctions among leadership styles—autocratic, democratic, laissez-faire, transactional, transformational, and situational. It is valuable to understand each of these styles and incorporate it into the work of a leader where appropriate, but we know that people are looking to their leader to provide a humanistic environment. Adept leaders understand that organizations are driven by people and never neglect the human element with it.

Unfortunately, traditional leadership training tends to close the door on servant-leadership's focus on the human element. But in our work, we have found that all leaders, with the correct guidance, can transform their leadership style to putting people first by allowing humanistic values and characteristics to shine.

We have found that adept leadership is outcomes-based. It is skillful, knowledgeable, visionary, and capable of executing a plan that will provide high-performance outcomes. Furthermore, an adept leader exercises good judgment and is collaborative and inclusive in the decision-making process.

At the same time, an adept leader provides a humanistic approach to the position and overtly demonstrates empathy for those they lead. Leaders who empathize and are sensitive to the needs of those on the front lines have a greater chance of leading more effectively. These leaders lead with heart but at the same time do not compromise the mission at hand. Adept leaders must nurture great loyalty and a passion for excellence.

Since everyone in an organization with adept leaders feels valued, respected, safe, and trusted, they expend a great deal of energy in working toward the organization's common goal. Whether implementing a new math or reading program, participating in contract negotiations, or dealing with a personnel issue, the people in the organization are less anxious handling difficult issues where a strong emotional quotient prioritizes staff.

Adept leaders also recognize that children do indeed come first but know that the members of the organization are equally important.

Consider the following strategies to adopting adept leadership.

- First and foremost, understand your role as a leader in creating high-performance outcomes and how as a leader will you facilitate this process.
- Review your responses from the organizational reflections in chapter 5.
- Examine the disconnections in the organization as revealed from the administration of the cross-check in appendix B, as well as the organizational-document findings, to develop a plan for remediation.
- Devise a strategy to listen to stakeholder concerns: assign liaisons to departments to listen, problem solve, provide perspective, and obtain feedback.
- Reexamine opportunities for employee engagement, satisfaction, and motivation.
- Consider the Fish! Philosophy: be there, play, make their day, choose your attitude.[3]
- Examine the worksheets in appendix A, activities #6 through 29.

ESSENTIAL IDEAS

- Execution is not merely tactics; rather, it is discipline and system.
- Successful implementation strategies are collaborative and empowering and engage all stakeholders.
- Strategic implementation requires ownership of all aspects of the plan.
- All members of a school or district are accountable to its outcomes.
- When self-reflection and assessment intersect with collaboration and achievement-related strategies, higher performance is inevitable.
- Good enough is not good enough!

Chapter Nine

Case Studies

CASE STUDY #1: REACHING ABOVE AND BEYOND

Several months after I assumed the superintendent's position, my school district entered into contract negotiations. While not rare, the dynamics involving the negotiations represented anything but the normal order. The school board was heavily invested into implementing an arbitrator's decision regarding a merit-pay provision from a previous contract. The plan known as "pay for performance" had been developed in conjunction with a highly regarded local university with funding assistance from the state's Department of Education.

In theory, the pay-for-performance plan was to recognize individual teachers and other staff members for improving student performance. In conjunction with university advisors, a formula with twenty-six variables was developed to compute a numerical value for each teacher. Those teachers with statistically significant values representing improved student achievement were awarded a small bonus. Other staff members whose achievement values could not be generated were eligible for a bonus after the analysis of soft data from a parent survey.

Almost immediately, the community and teachers questioned the reliability of the results. Most board members were publicly steadfast in their support for merit pay but privately questioned whether this particular program was the best approach. Teachers further decried the program's divisive nature and its failure to recognize the collaborative and collegial components of the teaching profession.

The teachers' association indicated that a contract settlement was contingent on the contract's removal of pay for performance. In a moment of exasperation, both the board president and the teacher association president pleaded with me to resolve the stalemate.

Understanding the history behind the school board's migration to merit pay was a starting point. Additionally, recognizing the staff's and board's positive contributions and initiatives, often ineffective and status quo oriented, was also important.

The school board was seeking to dramatically improve student achievement in an underperforming district, while teachers, in their attempt to remove merit pay, were seeking validation as professionals who knew how to improve achievement levels—this despite there never having been so far a coordinated teacher effort demonstrating improved results. My challenge was to find a balance between both the board's and the teachers' association's perspectives.

From the outset it was obvious that the district required a more strategic approach in its efforts to improve student achievement. Not unlike a majority of districts or schools suffering from piecemeal problem solving, this district often sought a program as a solution to a problem or created an initiative in response to an issue without ever conducting their due diligence regarding effectiveness.

Programs had been layered on top of existing programs with the hope that new programs and initiatives would produce the desired improvement in student achievement. Even though the organization had floundered over many years in the delivery of improved student outcomes, the overall alignment of the organization was never examined. Increased local and state funding resulted in the same stagnant outcomes.

Untangling the interconnected web of ineffective programs, marginally productive instructional practices, and status quo traditions required that I begin a dialogue with the board and the teachers' association concerning its mission, values, and practices and that I ascertain where those beliefs and values were prevalent in the organization. Simple questions—What do we believe, value, practice, and measure?—framed the conversation. Eventually a common language and concept was agreed upon that assisted in creating a framework for improvement.

From this dialogue, a district improvement plan emerged, known as Reaching Above and Beyond. The plan often described as a school-achievement model merged the concepts of continuous improvement and synergistic alignment to dramatically improve achievement. It was ambitious and far-reaching, and it contained longitudinal and short-range plans for improvement.

Simultaneously, as plans were being implemented, a vision and philosophy for improvement that would drive the organization was implemented at every instructional and operational level. By aligning a rigorous curriculum model with an accountability model that collaboratively developed district and building goals with a system of checks and balances, and by providing a group monetary award based on goal attainment, the district worked as a unified team for the benefit of its student body. Staff were furthered empowered through a career-ladder and master-teacher program. Almost immediately our state-assessments results started to move in a positive direction.

Over a number of years, the district's test scores placed it at the top of the county in many achievement categories. As a result of its dramatic turnaround, the district was recognized as a regional leader in the area of student achievement.

We continually attempted to recruit and retain the best, instill a philosophy of continuous improvement, nurture a belief that attitude equals altitude, and model an aptitude for twenty-first-century leadership, but the key to our success was recognizing that the journey was never complete.

The very concept of continuous improvement demands that a school or district never be complacent. While accomplishments were celebrated and those who provided leadership were recognized, we also took a page from history. Clearly, we recognized, once an organization rests on its laurels, entrenchment and stagnation follow shortly thereafter. To remain the best and to maintain excellence, a leader must have the aptitude to keep what works, tweak it, and be open to effective change.

CASE STUDY #2: FRAMING THE FUTURE

Upon assuming my career as superintendent of schools, I wanted to learn more about the district in general. During the hiring process, I had heard tales of the "fiasco" that was the previous strategic-planning process, which had included multiple committees and hundreds of work hours by all involved.

Despite the commitment of all those involved in the process, the board of education never adopted the entire plan and never implemented the approved components of the plan. Unfortunately, the board's action generated a great deal of frustration, anger, distrust, and apathy toward any type of district initiative, let alone enthusiasm for any further planning for the future. Since a strategic plan was again due as a requirement of state code, I decided to further gather information from stakeholders about the previous process.

The president of the teachers' association informed me that he would do anything possible to support the work of the district *except* participate in another strategic-planning process. His feelings were shared by many in the district.

Resentments over the prior process lingered throughout the district. Other discussions with colleagues revealed that most districts experience similar issues during the strategic-planning process: the process usually begins with great hope, lots of volunteers joining in, only to be culminated in a series of broken promises and goals largely ignored.

According to Bossidy and Charan, a strategic plan should:

- "clearly lay out in specific terms the direction of the organization—where it is now, where it will be going, and how it will get there," and "provide a set of directions much like a road map, 'lightly filled in,'" in that it allows plenty of room to maneuver,"
- as well as "identify that the strategy belongs to the leader rather than . . . a consultant or facilitator; a leader takes responsibility for the construction of the plan and gets some help, and then—when everyone agrees with the strategy—he/she assumes responsibility for developing action plans."[1]

After spending over thirty years in public education and taking part in six strategic plans from the classroom level to the superintendent's office, and experiencing some of the same frustrations, our team was determined not to repeat past mistakes. We started by working with the board of education and the cabinet leadership to set the stage for the next strategic plan and to develop a process that would ensure the development of a plan to position the schools for the future—and a plan that would actually be implemented. We had to be reasonable in our expectations, though, because previously a lack of fiscal responsibility had doomed plans from the outset.

With this in mind, our administrative team strategized what we termed a "living plan" that would generate the lost enthusiasm and trust. Most importantly, the plan would ultimately improve learning for all students in the district. To understand the process, administrators and employee leaders at an expanded retreat participated in:

- a study of the Baldrige Strategic-Planning process and of districts that had been recognized for quality
- the development of initial recommendations that included a list of sequential steps with logical time lines, a decision-making process, a list of stakeholders, plans for surveys, and criteria on how to effectively implement the plan
- the formation of a strategic-planning committee to guide the development process
- and the training of cabinet members on how to create a futures conference as the culminating event of the strategic-planning process.

Key to the development of our new strategic plan were:

- the creation of a strategic-planning committee, comprised of staff, board, and community members, to shape a meaningful, viable planning process

- a strategic overview to all 2,100 employees as part of an opening convocation, which provided opportunities for input
- an evening community forum to share information about the process and obtain feedback
- the completion of comprehensive surveys—which we titled "Framing the Future"—to acquire additional feedback from a broader audience, including students in grades 4 through 12
- and strategic review days, which included leadership teams from all buildings and departments, designed to solicit feedback on effective programs and current needs.

At the culminating event in the process, the two-day futures conference, key community stakeholders, employee leaders, and students analyzed the four key goals and suggested actions for each. The conference unfolded, filled with enthusiasm and eye-opening feedback from students sharing what it was like to be a student in the twenty-first century. As unprecedented camaraderie and trust developed between parents, community leaders, staff, and students, follow-up meetings were scheduled to communicate the group's progress.

The conference had been designed by a planning committee over a six-month period. During the two days it was held, participants:

- reviewed the goals, progress, accomplishments, and unfinished business from the previous plan
- synthesized the information from surveys, input, and strategy review days
- learned about the forces shaping the future of education and implications for the twenty-first century
- studied external global trends
- and listened to a presentation—A View from the Bridge—in which the superintendent reviewed strategic challenges confronting the district.

The entire process resulted in our establishing stretch goals that would position our school district in the top 5 percent of school districts in Pennsylvania, as measured by state-assessment scores, and set us up to achieve an outstanding rating from students, parents, and staff for a safe, orderly, and healthy environment. Additionally, it was important that each department in our district achieve organizational excellence through collaboration, exemplary outcomes, and fiscal responsibility. These goals provided the foundation for both the present and the future.

To eliminate the failures of the past, My One-Page Plan, as I call it (see appendix C), provided a system of accountability to ensure that all goals and action steps were implemented and completed.

In the end, this process, which embedded the concepts of alignment, accountability, positive attitude for growth, and reliance on leadership's aptitude to manage change and continuous improvement, drove the district toward world-class outcomes and world-class status.

CASE STUDY #3: RAISING THE BAR

We were hired as consultants to assess a very distressed school district. Located in the western Great Plains, the school district was small and rural, with a history of rich cultural traditions and community pride. The community's support of the district was evidenced by its willingness to invest in numerous initiatives, technology, and incentives for staff. The board expressed a strong interest in moving from the status quo of underperformance to creating increased learning opportunities that would maximize each student's potential.

Commendations and Challenges

While obvious challenges arose from the district's size, isolation, limited funding, and teacher-retention issues and from the complexity of reporting to two governmental organizations, it also became evident that the school district had the internal capacity to improve incrementally toward organizational effectiveness.

The district had already implemented various initiatives, programs, and components to improve effectiveness. And its pride, passion, and desire to improve were evident in the interviews we conducted with board members, the leadership team, teachers, parents, support staff, and other school stakeholders. The improvement of the district's student performance would require an assessment of its alignment, atmosphere, accountability systems, and leadership.

Assessment Process

Prior to our consultant-team's arrival to the district, we'd had board members, the superintendent, the leadership team, and teachers complete a school systems cross-check evaluation. The survey examined four key elements to an effective organization—alignment, atmosphere and attitude, accountability, and adept leadership. Survey participants were provided an opportunity to clarify responses.

Interviews were conducted with several school stakeholder groups with the purpose of further clarifying survey responses. Additionally, through the interview process consultants attempted to cross-validate responses between survey groups.

Another component of the cross-check was to audit district documents and policies to determine their impact on practices along with the consistency with which these practices were executed.

Statement of the Problem

Based on a state's assessment, school-district performance in reading, mathematics, and language was significantly below the state average. The district's academic performance and student-retention rates at that time had the potential of limiting student postsecondary and career options and might expose students to the detrimental impact of various social and emotional issues. The district's current performance was the antithesis of the district's vision—for all students to be college-bound or career ready upon graduation.

The school's board of directors had expressed its commitment to reversing the downward trend in student performance and student-retention rates; in fact, they were the ones who had initiated the dialogue about continuous improvement. It was our sense that the board of directors, superintendent, administrative-leadership team, and teachers believed that all children can learn and succeed.

A segment of the stakeholders, from direct experience, felt a sense of hopelessness from the continued lack of improvement. But it was our belief that the district had the internal fortitude to improve, overcome obstacles, and strategically plan with all stakeholders accordingly to make incremental gains on its journey toward excellence.

Evaluation Instrument: School Systems Cross-Check

The school systems cross-check instrument examines the interconnection of school and district processes and programs by cross-checking the embedded performance of key elements in vital organizational areas. The evaluation instrument attempts to research an organization for the existence of those elements, search for distinct demonstrations of the elements, and make recommendations based on instrument data. Participants in the survey ranked the prevalence or strength of each element—alignment, atmosphere/attitude, accountability, and adept leadership.

Findings

Overall, the school systems cross-check survey identified disconnections between the superintendent, board members, principals, leadership-team members, and teachers regarding the prevalence or strength of the four organizational elements (see table).

As illustrated in the table, the prevalence or strength of each organizational element among survey groups ranged from a low of 55 percent to a high of

Four-Element Prevalence Chart

	Alignment	Atmosphere	Accountability	Adept leadership
Leadership team	78%	63%	76%	78%
Teachers	62%	55%	63%	61%

78 percent. There were also wide discrepancies among survey groups regarding the effectiveness of the strategic plan, district goals, expectations, values, support systems, evaluations, professional development, teamwork, modeling, and leadership styles. Survey groups identified district outcomes, individual and collective accountability, buy-in, mentoring and coaching, new-teacher skills, professional-development programs, curriculum linkage, and parent and community participation as low.

Interviews

Interviews were conducted with all survey groups to clarify information from the evaluation instrument and to discuss areas of concern. The issues highlighted by the interviews included:

- student achievement
- attendance
- accountability
- climate/culture/relationships
- communication
- family and community engagement
- clarity of goals
- organizational effectiveness
- effective strategic planning
- special-education practices
- social/emotional/behavioral issues
- and technology.

More specifically, student proficiency levels, graduation rates, attendance, and student discipline were considered major issues. The climate was described as divisive and lacking unity of purpose, but at the same time there was a desire to improve communication and parent–school connections through community outreach.

Commentary regarding curriculum focused on rigor, relevance, the lack of electives, technical training, and teaching methodologies. Disciplinary issues were also linked to the limitations of the instructional program.

Beyond instructional issues associated with student discipline, procedural and programmatic issues contributed to the disciplinary referral process with the lack of options and behavioral support staff.

Both the school systems cross-check evaluative instrument and the interview process highlighted confusion regarding goals and action plans. Internal processes and procedures that involved the special-education referral process, technology, and the internal complaint procedures appeared to interfere with organizational effectiveness.

A significant level of concern was reported regarding new-teacher recruitment, new-teacher skill level, professional development, support systems, and retention rates.

Document Review and Analysis

From a review and analysis of district documents and practices, it is evident that the school district had invested resources and human capital in the development of policies, practices, and programs in its search to provide a quality instructional-learning environment. The review also verified the disconnectedness documented by the school systems cross-check instrument with the overarching elements of alignment, atmosphere/attitude, accountability, and adept leadership.

The review of documents and practices revealed several general problems:

- confusion regarding priorities, goals, and action plans
- the lack of metrics for measuring program effectiveness
- and inconsistency in the implementation of core practices and policies.

The aforementioned is evidenced by the multitude of goals listed in the five-year plan, school-wide goals, S.M.A.R.T. goals, and building goals without well-defined action plans for implementation and metrics for the evaluation of goals. Additionally, layers of educational theory, standards, and other initiatives require further examination for their effectiveness and further analysis of those layers in the context of teacher turnover.

Our goal was to assist the district focus in establishing priorities and in determining program effectiveness. The school district had a solid foundation, so when priorities were identified, well-defined action plans developed, and the instructional dots connected, incremental progress would be sure to occur. An effective strategic plan that aligns vision, mission, core values, measurable goals, action plans, and specific targets for improvements can assist with the improvement process.

Discussion

Despite the extent and nature of the issues in the district, it is our belief that the school district had the internal capacity to incrementally meet its targeted outcomes. Clearly wide discrepancies in organizational effectiveness existed between the administration, leadership team, and teaching staff.

Certainly some of these discrepancies had contributed to the district's performance levels and had dramatically impacted the overall atmosphere in the district. Through the implementation of a collaborative and inclusive continuous-improvement model capitalizing on the district's rich cultural history, incorporating community stakeholders into the process, and mobilizing its resources in an effective manner, we believed that the district possessed the human capital to succeed.

Recommendations

Changing a culture of teaching and learning required making decisions about when and where to institute reforms. In our experience, the most profound changes are generally implemented at entry levels, as they create momentum for future long-term growth.

This report discussed a significant number of organizational elements and indicators that ultimately impacted performance and instruction in the school district. Some of these elements required a more systemic (long-term) treatment, while others required reexamination.

For the purposes of the report and to expedite the improvement process, recommendations were classified by priority for implementation. For example, immediate priorities were those in need of implementation prior to the opening of school, while short-term recommendations were initiatives whose planning could commence in the fall. Long-term recommendations required extensive research or reallocation of funds and, therefore, were delayed for implementation in the following year.

Immediate Priorities

District Goals

It was essential that a consensus be reached regarding the district's instructional goals. No more than four major goals were suggested, which drove the development of building goals. Action plans developed in a collaborative manner from the superintendent's office to the classrooms included measurable targets, to be communicated in a transparent manner throughout the district, monitored, and adjusted throughout the year, the results being reported to the board and community.

Communication

All stakeholders in the organization needed to understand the identified deficiencies and priorities and plan to rectify them. It is our experience that it is essential, when structuring a communication plan that is ongoing, to internalize the goals of the workforce and to continually reinforce the values and mission of the organization to which they were aligned.

Student Discipline

Consistency in the application of discipline was essential for a successful school year. All teachers had to understand the importance of consistency in the application of the discipline code and had to understand the entire referral process. A team approach utilizing all behavioral options, district resources, and community services had to be incorporated into the intervention process. (Other recommendations in this area were found in the report's short-term and long-term initiatives.)

Observation, Supervision, and Evaluation

Prior to the opening of school, all staff members had to clearly understand instructional expectations, guidelines for professional conduct, and the observation and supervision process.

The previous model did not appear to have yielded the necessary formative feedback for teacher skill development. Prior to the opening of the year or shortly thereafter, it is important that a formative model be reviewed with staff and implemented. In our district, building principals and other personnel who conduct observations needed to clearly understand the expectations and be accountable to implement the process as designed.

Professional Orientation

Besides understanding of the current instructional nonnegotiables, teachers needed to receive direct, basic instruction on the fundamental operational aspects of the district from district leaders, concerning administration, business, technology, grade-level leaders, and special education, in addition to the district reference manual. In addition, each staff member was assigned a mentor or coach for support.

Developing an Understanding of Culture

A foundation regarding the importance of connecting the district's culture to curriculum was necessary to assist teachers in creating greater instructional relevancy. (See the section on short-term recommendations in the following for additional information.)

Community Outreach

For sustainable change, it was necessary to reach out and seek the assistance of community leaders. The school and community had to stand united in their efforts to educate the students. It was suggested that community leaders and parents attend not only the opening school ceremonies but also participate in school orientation programs for students regarding discipline and other related topics in an attempt to present a united, collaborative front as the district began to initiate various changes.

Short-Term Recommendations

Student Achievement

Factors contributing to low student proficiency included curriculum rigor, methodology, low expectations, student attendance, and student behavior. Therefore, reading and writing and mathematics were priorities in developing short-term building goals, and, therefore, specific considerations were incorporated into the action-plan framework:

- Rigor—require comparative and inferential responses as part of both classroom and homework assignments.
- Relevance—increase the number of project-based assignments that integrate multiple disciplines (i.e., reading, mathematics, science, and technology).
- Methodology—require the utilization of engagement strategies that are interactive, deductive/constructivist, manipulative, and technological.
- Writing—require a writing-across-the-curriculum program with the implementation of portfolios for each student by grade and subject.
- Test-taking skills—embed skills in the daily instructional program rather than in stand-alone activities.

Other considerations included:

- the coordination of new reading and math programs
- data analysis of skill-level performance (drilling down beyond the percentages)
- and developing a "triage" student list of high-risk underachievers, detailing the interventions to be undertaken with each.

Developing an Understanding of the Culture

The interview process revealed a need to incorporate training to assist in understanding the dynamics of how the children are socialized both into their home culture and into the school culture. A study or research group would then provide best practices and instructional resources of relevant methods and activities for utilization in the classroom. Finding connections in the curriculum to reflect the culture of the students can help create meaning for students who often do not see school meaningful or reflective of their culture.

Student Discipline

Upon examination of disciplinary data, it appeared that there were chronic offenders at the elementary level and chronic offenders at the high school level. There were also concerns about a concentration of behavioral issues in the seventh grade. In the planning process, the team entertained these specific considerations:

- intervention plans for chronic offenders were established as needed
- support services were examined, especially the effectiveness of special-education services (i.e., identification of students, IEP adherence, child-study teams, functional behavioral analysis, and so on)
- and security protocols and student supervision were established.

Attendance

Poor attendance contributed to low achievement and high dropout rates. While addressing curriculum relevance and school connectedness, support programs were necessary to reverse the disappointing trends in the district. A planning team looking to improve their school must further examine the effectiveness of home and school-visitor procedures, the application of the home-visit requirement, and the utilization of technology in the notification process. Transition classes should be considered so as to eliminate reteaching.

Accountability

Accountability across all levels was essential to our district's improvement and will be for any other district looking to make improvements. Consider adjusting the current principal-evaluation system to reflect current initiatives and personal goals. The district may want to consider a master-teacher program to recognize excellence, build teacher leadership, and increase retention.

Communication

To reestablish a positive atmosphere and culture in the school district, it appeared necessary to analyze the effectiveness of the entire communication program and to consider greater stakeholder involvement. It was suggested that team members incorporate specific elements into their comprehensive plan:

- positive messaging
- technology utilization (like volo [a robotic caller recorded messaging], texting, etc.)
- distribution of data
- promoting transparency
- and greater cultural integration.

Recruitment and Retention

The recruitment and retention of highly skilled staff members had been an ongoing challenge for the school district. The 2016 and 2017 school year alone required the replacement of half of its teachers and two principals. The continuous burden of retraining staff and the underlying issue of student-teacher trust had hindered relationship building. Planning team members needed to consider:

- using job fairs, Teach For America, Troops to Teachers, Bureau of Indian Education advertisement services, SpringBoard, and other such programs as resources
- appointing mentors, coaches, and other department leaders with associated stipends
- and advertising for a behavioral therapist support position.

Long-Term Recommendations

A framework of continuous improvement and a philosophy that all children can learn and succeed needed to guide the school district in its long-term decision-making process. Some of the initiatives listed below for long-term consideration required outreach, reallocation of resources, and community collaboration.

alignment:

- annual program reviews with metrics

achievement:

- additional courses and electives
- independent study
- technical training
- grant opportunities

- Gates Scholarships
- STEM Academies
- AVID–like programming (contracts, study/organizational support structures)

attendance:

- regional-court collaboration
- mental-health and drug and alcohol services/SADD chapter

discipline:

- restorative practices
- "capturing kids hearts"
- response to intervention (RTI)
- behavioral options—alternative school
- services for emotionally disturbed students
- regional cooperative agency support

activities:

- greater programming
- increased school-related summer programming
- college visitations

atmosphere, attitude, and culture:

- comprehensive communication plan
- cultural outreach
- cultural programming—language, art, etc.

accountability:

- systemic program
- due-process procedures
- complaint investigation

ESSENTIAL IDEAS

- Untangling the interconnected web of ineffective programs, marginally productive instructional practices, and status quo traditions requires a problem-solving dialogue and a vision of the outcomes necessary to improve performance.

- The continuous-improvement process demands that a school or district is always moving forward and guards against complacency.
- Leaders must have the aptitude to keep what works, tweak other areas in need of attention, and be willing to facilitate real change.
- Performance goals must be an organizational stretch but at the same time allow for incremental growth.
- Growth is not an overnight process but rather one that reflects immediate, short-term. and long-range goals.

Conclusion

WHY HIGH PERFORMANCE?

In this book, we have presented the process to begin the journey to high performance by suggesting four critical areas that need to be addressed, provided reflective questions to guide the evaluation of your status, and detailed a menu of proven strategies that can be utilized to address each of these areas within the unique context of your school or district. These four critical elements show us how to follow the road to better performance. However, to ensure success we feel that it is imperative that we share why we were motivated to strive for excellence.

Knowing what to improve and how to do it is important, but the road to better performance is not without its twists, turns, and bumps that, unfortunately, discourage many leaders. Without the internal drive, motivation, and moral imperative to tackle these important issues, a leader's success will be limited.

Larry Lezotte reminds us that this work is not for the faint of heart.[1] So, after outlining the key components in the process in the previous chapters, our concluding chapter is why we ought to strive for higher performance, first considering the big picture, and then zeroing in on individual motivations that pushed us to start and lead this journey.

THE BIG PICTURE

Asking why you should embark on a journey toward higher performance is really asking "Why not?"

According to the National Center for Education Statistics, as of the fall of 2017, approximately 50.7 million students are enrolled in public elementary and secondary schools nationwide.[2] And based on the National Assessment of Education Progress (NAEP), a substantial number of those students are performing at a basic and below-basic proficiency level.[3] These results have continued to remain stagnant through 2017. While clearly those performance levels are reflective of the changing demographics in the country, a status quo strategy or a series of ineffective initiatives randomly formulated at an attempt to solve those issues will only produce, at best, a system of mediocre schools.

NAEP, long considered the gold standard in assessment, annually gathers representative achievement samples from over seven hundred thousand students. Based on the results from their 2013 assessment, "60 percent of students in California, Texas, Florida, New York, and Illinois, often called mega states due to size of public school enrollment in those states, performed at the basic and below-basic level."[4] Similar results are found in practically every state across the country. Even more disturbing, a Brookings Institution study showed little change in the trajectory in math and virtually no progress in reading from 2005 to 2015.[5]

Whether you are an advocate for or opponent of the standardized-testing process, it is difficult to deny that there isn't a student-achievement issue. Simply ask a teacher what percentage of their students has the ability to solve complex problems, reason abstractly, draw inferences, and write proficiently. You may be surprised at the answer.

The impact of these low proficiency levels is far-reaching, and unless dramatic improvement in those levels occurs, the impact on our future is profound. Our global competitiveness, our economic stability, our stature as a world leader, and even our national security may be compromised unless our national resolve is harnessed to solve the issue of poor student achievement.

So, why work for higher achievement? It's a matter of moral responsibility for the citizens of this great nation. To allow what was once considered the greatest education system in the world to slip from our grasp is to let the foundation of our democracy and our fundamental greatness disappear.

Over thirty years ago in the nationally acclaimed study *A Nation at Risk*, John Goodlad described "the decline of our educational system in detail, but in many ways those warnings went unheeded."[6] Since that time, the obstacles, barriers, and socioeconomic variables in turning the tide from low to high achievement have become increasingly complex, but as a country we have always soared in the face of adversity.

All too often we have become content with the status quo or have applied an ineffective quick-fix solution to a very complex problem. These approaches often silenced vocal constituency groups, but, what with the leveling of the international playing field, status quo thinking, ineffective strategies, quick fixes, and our inability to embrace collective accountability will relegate our schools to second-class status. Even the touted turnaround reforms have shown themselves to not be silver bullets.[7]

So a second response to why we should aim for higher-performing schools is that equity is a concern. All children should have access to a school system that supports effective organizational strategies and methodologies and be in the care of twenty-first-century leadership capable of producing outcomes that maximize student potential.

Despite the obstacles and impediments to success, real twenty-first-century leaders always find a way to implement systemic change that produce high-level outcomes. It is about a team of teams that understands the vision and mission, a team aligned with that vision, but also a team in an interconnected system of transparency and shared consciousness.[8]

In the end there is no why but rather why not—because we have the collective inherent internal capacity to make a difference now for the sake of all children and this great country.

OUR PERSONAL MOTIVATION AND JOURNEY

As for the two of us, the question as to why our districts were driven to strive for higher performance really never entered our minds. If given the premise of high performance, more thought, our response would also have been, "Why not?"

Having been involved in sports and extracurricular activities throughout our entire careers, it was a natural and logical progression to strive for excellence in our profession too. We know of no team, band, or competitive organization that prepares without the goal of being the best.

So why should an educational system be any different? Few groups ever experience what it feels like to be the champion, but all strive to reach the pinnacle of their chosen endeavor. We owe it to our students, our community, and our country to plan, to work, and to strive for higher-performing schools. Our students must be prepared to compete on a global stage.

At the time in our careers when we were superintendents, our districts, like many districts through our country, had much room for improvement. Both of the school districts we superintended were held in high esteem, especially by those who worked within them and, for the most part, by the community.

In both cases, our facilities were excellent, the environment was safe, and the funding revenues good. Employees worked hard, took pride in their work, and believed that they were extremely successful. However, as we began to look more closely at our performance indicators, the disaggregated data demonstrated that, while, overall, our systems were relatively effective, they were not providing an equitable education for all of our students.

In one district, while many key leaders were satisfied with the national percentile ranking of the district, the school board president felt strongly that many children, particularly those considered average and below average, were not achieving at acceptable levels. In the other district, board members dissatisfied with student outcomes and administrative initiatives unilaterally adopted a series of ineffective programs to improve student achievement.

In both cases, board members perceived that school tax monies were not producing the desired results and decreed that, as "guardians of tax dollars," the district should be more effective in the utilization of revenue to educate their children. Further examination clearly revealed disconnects between achievement outcomes and the districts' missions, values, policies, procedures, and program effectiveness.

At the same time, upon seeking feedback from employees, we found that most did not feel valued. Often, these feelings resulted from previously negotiated contractual agreements, conflicting expectations, the failure to include employees in the decision-making process, and a perception that district funds were not being utilized properly. In both districts, faculty members worked in "silos," believing that their individual approach to teaching and learning was effective in producing the desired results.

With the knowledge that gaps in achievement existed between various groups of students and that dissatisfaction existed within the staff, board, and community, we discovered that our existing strategic plans had been developed without a clear and measurable direction. In addition, little attention was being given to a coordinated plan for staff development designed to increase employee capacity and to address district deficiencies.

Like most districts, both of our districts had strong parent involvement. However, authentic parent and community engagement did not exist. In each of our districts, benchmark data was either nonexistent or ignored as a tool for improvement.

With a myriad of data yet to analyze and no shortage of advice on what direction to take, it was necessary that we recognize the accomplishments of the past and, at the same time, begin a process of change. We knew that we had to change the beliefs and culture in each of our districts. In both districts, we began to create a sense of urgency by analyzing our current status while searching for educational research, philosophies, and exemplars that could move us toward greater performance.

Many suggested that we should run our organizations more like a business, while others claimed that the business model could not be applied to our schools. We heard a plethora of excuses regarding our low performance:

"We are doing well considering the challenges that face the district."

"We need more resources and staff."

"We cannot expect more because parents just do not care or support our efforts."

"The strategic plan is a necessary evil that is never executed as intended. Its best function is as a doorstop."

"Until students take responsibility for themselves, we cannot do much better."

"Our board just gets in the way. They do not support and respect educators."

"Just let me close the door and teach. I know what to do."

"We always did it this way, and it seems to work."

"The administrators and board have no idea what we deal with every day."

"Now they want me to examine data. I don't have any more time in my day."

Interestingly, our two boards viewed the concept of continuous improvement differently. In one district, the continuous-improvement process was perceived as having the potential to expose systemic flaws that could be utilized against them for political gain in the next election. In another, the board embraced the concept of improvement as a political means of making a statement to the public regarding the effectiveness of the board.

While teacher unions and associations were often willing to embrace the concept of continuous improvement, it was clear that any improvement process and particularly any system of accountability could only be accomplished with their direct involvement.

Regardless of the reasons, we knew that the traditional command-and-control style of leadership needed to be replaced with a collaborative model of leadership that built a team approach. We knew that we had to capitalize on the good work of our staff and create the conditions to move their practice from those individual silos to an organizational team effort. We needed to create a networked system in which each individual assumed responsibility for the success or failure of the group. And, most importantly, we recognized that it was our responsibility to put aside a hierarchical approach and lead through ongoing self-assessment without being reluctant to look at our personal strengths and weaknesses.

We provided opportunities to listen and to respond to our constituents and to immerse ourselves in knowing our organizations. Recognizing the complexity of the improvement and change process and the number of moving parts, constituent groups, time lines, and the this-is-how-we've-always-done-it mentality, it was obvious that the road to higher performance was going to be a bumpy journey.

Underlying our desire to move our districts to higher performance was always a question of whether we could deliver on our promise. It was a volatile question with a great deal of personal risk on our part, given the number of variables that needed to be addressed.

Many superintendents would be reluctant to put themselves on the line to delineate measurable achievement goals, knowing the dramatic growth that would be required. Nonetheless, we believed that with the proper alignment, a system of accountability, an atmosphere of improvement, and adept collaborative leadership we could achieve our goals. Clearly, this was not going to occur overnight—or even in a year or two.

Being able to openly communicate that this improvement would require growth longitudinally, horizontally, and vertically at the same time was key. It would require the utilization of data, internal assessments, surveys, communication, collaboration, and the mobilization of all the knowledge and talent within our two organizations. Most importantly, it would require a change of culture in how we approached teaching and learning for all children.

Changing a school or a district's culture is one of the most challenging steps in the school-improvement process, and it requires adept leadership to tackle it. When a school or district's culture is threatened by moving from the status quo, often asking why we should bother trying to improve takes center stage. When long-standing practices and policies are called into question, those members of the school and district tied to those practices and policies begin to question the initiative and even mobilize opposition to it. It is important to have the courage to face this opposition head-on, honestly, and in a thoughtful manner.

In recognizing those challenges and anticipating many other pitfalls, we scheduled opportunities for feedback from all constituents. We developed professional partnerships that provided access to nationally known speakers who addressed the challenge of striving to become excellent. These speakers and others informed us how to better utilize data, how to not only involve but also authentically engage the community, and how to establish a belief system in which it was clear that our priority was the learning of all children.

We also began to attend conferences that focused on continuous improvement and on how to align our system with our goals. We also found that the work of Larry Lezotte and his Correlates of Effective Schools provided an excellent starting point.[9] Lezotte's work provided a framework for us to challenge long-held belief systems and move us in the direction of continuous improvement. We also learned that alignment, accountability, atmosphere, and adept leadership can move any district to higher performance.

Our journey, which required strategic readjustment from time to time, caused us to recognize the importance of removing obstacles and roadblocks in building consensus. Through our experiences, our work, and our achievements, we know that every leader can take their organization on a journey toward higher performance.

In embarking on this journey it is imperative that you recognize that you cannot do it alone. You must be collaborative and inclusive and have the courage to face those defending the status quo with a moral imperative and rationale that is so compelling that the path to higher-performing schools is indisputable. If you are a relentless advocate for each and every student, you too can realize greater student and organizational performance!

Reaching the heights of becoming a high-performing school is a formidable challenge. Hopefully you are no longer asking why or why not but, rather, *when*.

Good luck on your journey to becoming a high-performing school or district!

ESSENTIAL IDEAS

- Higher performance for all schools and school districts is a moral imperative.
- All students can learn and succeed.
- School improvement is not for the faint of heart.
- All schools and districts have the collective internal capacity to make a difference in the lives of the children they serve.
- Achieving higher levels of performance is not an isolated endeavor.
- Changing a culture requires courage and savvy leadership.
- Higher performance is no longer a question of why or why not but rather a question of when!

IV

Appendixes

The appendixes attempt to provide a variety of activities and tools for practitioners and aspiring leaders so that they can sharpen their district's focus regarding alignment, atmosphere and attitude, accountability, and adept leadership.

These activities are designed to provide opportunities for group collaboration, inclusionary discussion, and feedback as you discover the status of your school or district on a continuum of continuous improvement and to provide strategies as you develop a plan for high-performance outcomes.

Appendix A

Activity Worksheets

ACTIVITY #1, ALIGNMENT

INSTRUCTIONS: In the areas indicated below, list your school or district's *vision*, *beliefs*, and *mission*. For each, specify *where* in the organization evidence exists that the vision is clearly demonstrated and *how* those demonstrations are best measured.

	Vision for your organization	Where is it in evidence?	How can it be measured?
(1)			
(2)			
(3)			

	Beliefs of your organization	Where are they in evidence?	How can they be measured?
(1)			

(2)

(3)

| Mission of your organization | Where is it in evidence? | How can it be measured? |

(1)

(2)

(3)

ACTIVITY #2, ALIGNMENT

INSTRUCTIONS: In the following, list a *policy* or *program*, its designed *outcome*, and its *effectiveness* regarding student achievement.

	Policy or program	Outcome	Effectiveness
(1)			
(2)			
(3)			
(4)			
(5)			
(6)			

ACTIVITY #3, ATMOSPHERE: ATMOSPHERIC BAROMETER

INSTRUCTIONS: Define each of the five categories listed below. On the blank line next to each category, rank each on the percentage of staff in your school or department who exhibit the listed quality. Average your scores.

Shared values ____

Attitudinal mind-set ____

Collaboration ____

Empowerment ____

Leadership ____

Average ____

ACTIVITY #4, ACCOUNTABILITY

INSTRUCTIONS: With your school or district's accountability program in mind, respond to the following prompts.

Define the goal or purpose of your accountability program.

What aspects of the program have been successful?

What aspects have been unsuccessful?

What obstacles has it presented?

ACTIVITY #5, ACCOUNTABILITY: SYSTEM-COMPONENT CHECKLIST

INSTRUCTIONS: Examine your school or district's accountability program, and determine whether or not the following components are part of it.

Summative
Formative
Inclusive
Collaborative
Data sources

- Standardized
- Benchmarks
- Indicators
- Rubrics

Instructional
Individual
Transparent or visible
Outcome- or goal-based
Linkage

- Curriculum
- Professional development

Intervention procedures

ACTIVITY #6, ADEPT-LEADERSHIP PRACTICES

INSTRUCTIONS: **Respond to the following passage in the blank space provided.**

With a complex organization, leaders themselves can be a limiting factor. While human capacity for thought and action is astounding, it is never quite enough. If we simply worked more and tried harder, we reason, we could master the onslaught of information and "urgent" requirements. But of course we can't.

Author Dan Levitin explains: "In 2011, Americans took in five times as much information every day as they did in 1986—the equivalent of 175 newspapers. During our leisure time, not counting work, each of us processes 34 gigabytes or 100,000 words every day. The world's 21,274 television stations produce 85,000 hours of original programming every day, as we watch an average of 5 hours of television every day, the equivalent of 20 gigabytes of audio-video images."

Where once an educated person might have assumed she was at least conversant in relevant knowledge of a particular field of study, the explosion of information has rendered that assumption laughable.

One solution to information overload is to increase a leader's access to information, fitting him or her with two smartphones, multiple computer screens, and weekend updates. But the leader's access to information is not the problem. We can work harder, but how much can we actually take in?

Attention studies have shown that most people can thoughtfully consider only one thing at a time and that multitasking dramatically degrades our ability to accomplish tasks requiring cognitive concentration. Given these limitations, the idea that a "heroic leader" enabled with an ubernetwork of connectivity can simultaneously control a thousand marionettes on as many stages is unrealistic.

ACTIVITY #7, ADEPT-LEADERSHIP PRACTICES: DECISION MAKING

INSTRUCTIONS: List your school or district's *stakeholders* in the decision-making process; determine how you *engage* each stakeholder group, and specifically state the process utilized to get stakeholder *buy-in*.

Stakeholders

Engagement

Buy-in

ACTIVITY #8, ADEPT-LEADERSHIP PRACTICES: DECISION MAKING AND PROBLEM SOLVING

INSTRUCTIONS: This activity helps delineate key aspects of the decision-making process in a sequential, linear manner. In the following space provided, define the *problem*, identify the *givens* (nonnegotiables) to the problem, prioritize the *givens*, develop a plan that focuses the organization on the *priorities*, define the *urgency* surrounding the problem, explaining why it is important to focus on the specific problems.

Define the problem.

Identify the givens.

Prioritize the givens.

Focus on the priorities.

Define the urgency.

ACTIVITY #9, ADEPT-LEADERSHIP PRACTICES: PROBLEM SOLVING AND PROCESS STEPS

INSTRUCTIONS: With your school or district in mind, respond to the following prompts.

Identify an initiative you have implemented that had the desired outcome as designed.

Identify the process that you have utilized in the successful implementation of this program or initiative.

Identify an initiative you have implemented that had an unintended negative outcome from the design. Why did this happen?

Compare and contrast the two processes utilized.

ACTIVITY #10, ADEPT-LEADERSHIP PRACTICES: APTITUDE QUOTIENT (AQ)

INSTRUCTIONS: Adept leaders understand the importance of creating a culture of collaboration, providing opportunities for engagement from a cross-section of stakeholders, and empowering staff. How do you encourage each of the following?

Collaboration

Engagement

Inclusiveness

Empowerment

Appendix A

ACTIVITY #11, ADEPT-LEADERSHIP PRACTICES: TEAMWORK AND SYNERGY

INSTRUCTIONS: *Synergy* is defined as the interaction of two or more people to produce a combined effect greater than the sum of each person's individual work. Others may simply define it as outcomes resulting from teamwork. Answer the following questions as they apply to your school or district.

What does synergy look like?

What can leaders do to make synergy happen?

ACTIVITY # 12, ADEPT-LEADERSHIP PRACTICES: TEAMWORK

INSTRUCTIONS: Answer the following questions as they apply to your school or district.

What does *teamwork* mean? (List five key words.)

(1)

(2)

(3)

(4)

(5)

What does it look like?

What gets in the way of a team working together?

What could you do to develop a sense of teamwork?

ACTIVITY #13, ADEPT-LEADERSHIP PRACTICES: ARE LEADERS BORN OR MADE?

INSTRUCTIONS: The idea that leaders are born and that leadership traits are innate is an outdated notion unsupported by research. More than 150 years of experience in developing leaders show that the *art and science* of leading well hinges less on genes and common sense and more on training, tenacity, and supervised experience. Leadership-facilitating traits include drive, intelligence, motivation, integrity, and self-confidence, while leadership-inhibiting traits include argumentativeness, insensitivity, narcissism, fear of failure, perfectionism, and impulsivity. With this in mind, respond to the following prompts as they pertain to your school or district.

Select one of the above-mentioned leadership-facilitating traits that best describes you.

Select one of the above-mentioned leadership-inhibiting traits that you may be prone to.

What type of situation causes you to become negative?

How can you avoid it?

ACTIVITY #14, ADEPT-LEADERSHIP PRACTICES: COMMITMENT

INSTRUCTIONS: Adept leaders learn to make commitments to organizations, causes, and those they supervise. They identify personally with the mission and find meaning in staying the course when things get tough. The most effective commitments are based on intrinsic values, not external rewards. Wise leaders understand that hard work and sacrifice enhance commitment and that loyalty and commitment thrive when subordinates' primary needs are met. With your school or district in mind, answer the following questions.

What commitment have you made regarding student achievement, excellence, or quality?

If any, what commitment or support has the board or other guiding organization provided you?

What have they not provided? What do you need to do to obtain their commitment or support?

Appendix A

ACTIVITY #15, ADEPT-LEADERSHIP PRACTICES: NURTURING LEADERS

INSTRUCTIONS: Adept leaders will succeed if they master key leadership characteristics. Leaders should nurture characteristics and habits within their teams. These characteristics are (1) *self-governance*, which is internally directed and enables leaders to fully manage and motivate themselves, (2) a full understanding of the importance of learning each position well and a demonstrated commitment to *competence*, (3) inspiring unequivocal *loyalty*, (4) *honesty and forthrightness* when reporting information, (5) *judiciousness*, (6) assuming full *responsibility* and accountability when things go wrong, and (7) a willingness to act *proactively* to intervene in situations—not for personal gain, but to make the organization better. In the following, with your school or district in mind, rank in order of importance the seven leadership characteristics: self-governance, competence, loyalty, honesty/forthrightness, judiciousness, responsibility, and proactiveness. Then answer the question that follows.

(1)

(2)

(3)

(4)

(5)

(6)

(7)

How can you encourage these characteristics among your team? How does this approach build the culture and atmosphere of your organization?

ACTIVITY #16, ADEPT-LEADERSHIP PRACTICES: CHARACTER

INSTRUCTIONS: Adept leaders are credible and responsible. Credible leaders are consistent; they are ethical and moral at all times. It is the fabric of who they are. Although adherence to timeless ethical principles is important, the strongest leaders exude personal virtues—internally located character qualities. Adept leaders are models of courage and commitment. In the following, describe a moment when you demonstrated courage or commitment in your current position in your school or district.

ACTIVITY #17, ADEPT-LEADERSHIP PRACTICES: REFLECTIVE VISION

INSTRUCTIONS: Adept leaders master the art of visioning and have reflected a vision for the organization on three levels: (1) First, they hone a vision of *self as leader* that realistically incorporates both talents and vulnerabilities, (2) they expertly craft convincing *visions of those they supervise*, visions that buoy esteem and capitalize on the strengths of subordinates, and (3) they craft a *vision for the organization*, discerning a corporate image of what the organization can become that wins over subordinates and stimulates commitment and achievement. With your school or district in mind, respond to the following questions.

What vision do you have for yourself?

What vision do you have for your key followers?

What vision do you have for your organization?

How do these visions support the expectations of the organization?

ACTIVITY #18, ADEPT-LEADERSHIP PRACTICES: STRESSORS

INSTRUCTIONS: In order to perform well when a crisis strikes or controversy escalates, adept leaders must be prepared to handle the stress arising from a variety of situations. Effective leaders accurately appraise the issue, problem, or threat associated with a situation and develop problem-focused strategies. Adept leaders are able to respond effectively and in a logical, controlled manner. With your school or district in mind, respond to the following prompts.

Identify the stressors in your position.

Identify a crisis or challenge that you have experienced. How did you handle it? What did you rely upon in this situation?

Explain how you dealt with all constituent groups—students, parents, board members, police, press, and the overall community.

ACTIVITY #19, ADEPT-LEADERSHIP PRACTICES: BUILDING LOYALTY

INSTRUCTIONS: Adept leaders place the needs of others before their own (see the discussion of servant leadership in chapter 8). They enjoy loyalty from colleagues and others because they are consistently loyal first. They appreciate the fact that leading well is an act of sacrifice, that leading requires a sober acceptance of obligation to serve followers. With your school or district in mind, respond to the following prompts in the space provided.

Detail three ways a leader can build loyalty.

(1)

(2)

(3)

How does loyalty connect with the vision, mission, and beliefs of your organization?

How does a leader deal with an individual who hasn't bought into the system?

ACTIVITY #20, ADEPT-LEADERSHIP PRACTICES: A MIND-SET BASED ON SUCCESS

INSTRUCTIONS: Seasoned leaders appreciate the significance of preparation as a means to success. With your school or district in mind, respond to the following prompts.

As a leader, what does success mean to you?

How do you define success as an organization?

Identify five operational action terms that imply success.

(1)

(2)

(3)

(4)

(5)

What do you believe is necessary for you to be successful as a leader? How can you or the organization make them a reality?

ACTIVITY #21, ADEPT-LEADERSHIP PRACTICES: MODELING

INSTRUCTIONS: Adept leaders understand and accept the burden of visibility. Leaders appreciate the power of modeling and recognize that followers will learn more by watching than listening. Not only are leaders conscious of providing a congruent example for the larger organization, they also work at ensuring that their interpersonal behavior offers an example they want subordinates to replicate. These leaders do not pontificate but, rather, effectively communicate the direction of the organization. With your school or district in mind, answer the following questions.

What types of activities should an effective leader model?

In an organization that places student achievement as its priority, what type of activities should a leader model?

How does leading by example build a culture or atmosphere of a school or district?

ACTIVITY #22, ADEPT-LEADERSHIP PRACTICES: EMPATHY AND SUBSTANCE

INSTRUCTIONS: Beyond being intelligent and exhibiting job-related expertise, adept leaders must exude emotional intelligence. To lead effectively, a leader must demonstrate emotional self-awareness, self-motivation, and genuine empathy for others. It has been said that the most effective leaders know how to balance empathy, personalities, and technical expertise. The goal is to have both substance and the personality to motivate. With your school or district in mind, respond to the following prompts.

Think of those individuals in your professional life who have been effective both because they have mastered the technical aspects of the position and because they have the personality to motivate staff. (It is a rare breed in administration that can demonstrate both.) How were these individuals able to gain the respect of the staff?

Respond to the following: How were these individuals able to maximize student potential and hold staff accountable?

ACTIVITY #23, ADEPT-LEADERSHIP PRACTICES: DELEGATION AND ACCOUNTABILITY

INSTRUCTIONS: Adept leaders motivate others to perform. They empower others and micromanage less. Rather than utilizing a command-and-control, top-down philosophy, adept leaders build human capacity. They are confident enough to surround themselves with smart and capable subordinates willing to assume more responsibility. Real leaders can delegate and empower but hold individuals accountable. With your school or district in mind, respond to the following prompts.

Rank yourself on a scale of 1 to 10 in the following areas:
Delegation _____

Empowerment _____

Accountability _____

What are the components of an effective system of accountability?

ACTIVITY #24, ADEPT-LEADERSHIP PRACTICES: INCLUSIONARY PRACTICES

INSTRUCTIONS: Great leaders find a way to include all groups in the decision-making process. Unifying leaders create opportunities for involvement and interaction. The challenge of bringing all groups to the decision table is critical to the success of an organization. With your school or district in mind, respond to the following prompts.

Identify all constituent groups, and strategize how to include individuals in the decision process, the teaching and learning process, and the overall culture of the organization.

What are the challenges that you face in this process?

How do you plan to overcome these challenges?

How do you build greater transparency for your organization?

ACTIVITY #25, BECOMING A HIGH-PERFORMING SCHOOL OR DISTRICT: BUILDING CONSENSUS TO IMPROVE

INSTRUCTIONS: Understanding the urgency to improve student performance is part of the process in building consensus to address identified issues and obstacles. With your school or district in mind, respond to the following prompts.

How do you build a sense of urgency?

Identify sources of data for analysis.

How do you determine which members of the school, district, or community to empower or include?

ACTIVITY #26, BECOMING A HIGH-PERFORMING SCHOOL OR DISTRICT: INDICATORS OF SUCCESS

INSTRUCTIONS: What does it mean to be *high performing*? How will a school or district measure higher performance? This activity assists in facilitating the conversation by having you identify indicators of success within your school or district, then having you define how the identified indicators are measured and whether those indicators are currently present or not.

	Indicator of success	How is it measured?	Present or not?
(1)			
(2)			
(3)			
(4)			
(5)			
(6)			
(7)			

(8)

ACTIVITY #27, BECOMING A HIGH-PERFORMING SCHOOL OR DISTRICT

INSTRUCTIONS: With your school or district in mind, respond to the following prompts.

Identify the skills students will require in the twenty-first century.

(1)

(2)

(3)

(4)

(5)

Prioritize the identified skills.

(1)

(2)

(3)

(4)

(5)

How effective has your organization been in delivering those skills, on a scale of 1 to 5 (1 being most effective, 5 the least)?

Strategize in outline form on how you would plan to ensure that students will develop these identified skills.

ACTIVITY #28, BECOMING A HIGH-PERFORMING SCHOOL OR DISTRICT

INSTRUCTIONS: With your school or district in mind, identify the areas in each of the following categories that you would target.

Alignment

Accountability

Atmosphere

Adept leadership

Activity Worksheets

ACTIVITY #29, BECOMING WORLD-CLASS: THE PLANNING PROCESS

INSTRUCTIONS: Looking to your responses in activity #28, specify in the space provided a *time line* for completion for each of your *targets* for improvement, specifying their related remedial *activities or treatments*.

Time line	Target	Activity or treatment
Immediate		
Short-term (within a year)		
Long-term (more than a year)		

NOTES

For activities 13 through 24, I have drawn from the work of W. Brad Johnson and Gregory P. Harper, *Becoming a Leader the Annapolis Way: 12 Combat Lessons from the Navy's Leadership Laboratory* (New York: McGraw-Hill, 2004), on the specified pages: activity #13, p. 20; #14, p. 35; #15, pp. 57–63; #16, p. 69; #17, p. 91. #18, p. 111; #19, pp. 136–37; #20, p. 161; #21, p. 175; #22, p. 195; and #23, p. 226.

Activity #6 is based on the work of Daniel Levitan, "The Organized Mind: Thinking Straight in an Age of Information Overload," http://www.YouTube.com (Talks at Google, October 28, 2014).

Appendix B

School Systems Cross-Check

Exemplary Schools Organization

Building World Class Schools

PART 1, EVALUATION INSTRUMENT

INSTRUCTIONS: The school systems cross-check examines the interconnection of school and district processes and programs by cross-checking embedded performance threads in key organizational areas. The systems cross-check attempts to research an organization for the existence of those threads, search for clear demonstrations of the threads, and make recommendations that result in a more effective organization. Where indicated in the following, rank your responses to the questions in each of the four areas—alignment, atmosphere/attitude, accountability, and adept leadership. Each response should be ranked as high (3), moderate (2), or low (1). For example, a high (3) ranking would indicate a high prevalence of the cited characteristic, while, conversely, a low (1) ranking would indicate a low prevalence of the cited characteristic. *If an item is ranked 1, or low, the reviewer must provide an explanation for the rating.*

Alignment

GOAL: To align all practices, processes, and goals, from the boardroom to the classroom.

Atmosphere/Attitude

GOAL: To build a culture of teamwork, collaboration, and positive attitude that maximizes the talents of all employees in creating a high-performing organization.

Accountability

GOAL: To design a systemic, customized continuous-improvement model with measureable benchmark indicators and processes that monitor and adjust effectiveness.

Adept Leadership for the Twenty-First Century

GOAL: To develop a collaborative model which assists leaders in aligning all aspects of the organization to achieve World Class excellence and high performing schools.

Scoring

Conclusion

(*See separate report, attached.*)

Recommendation

(*See separate report, attached.*)

Alignment

(1) The district utilizes a comprehensive strategic plan as a framework for the organization's goals and aspirations. (1-2-3)

(2) The district has a process to review existing programs. (1-2-3)

(3) The district has developed realistic and measurable goals with time lines and monitoring checkpoints. (1-2-3)

(4) District goals are aligned with leadership goals at all levels. (1-2-3)

(5) The organization's values, beliefs, mission, and vision are ingrained in the culture of the district. (1-2-3)

(6) The district embraces a model for continuous improvement. (1-2-3)

(7) The district conducts comprehensive and targeted assessments to identify strengths and opportunities for improvement. (1-2-3)

(8) The district supports and articulates an internal assessment (or assessments) aligned to all goals, programs, and processes. (1-2-3)

Appendix B

(9) The instructional aspects of the organization are focused on solving student-achievement-related (SA) issues (policies, programs, student discipline, professional development, technology, pupil services, etc.). (1-2-3)

(10) The noninstructional aspects of the organization attempts to solve SA issues. (1-2-3)

(11) Continuous-improvement plans address SA issues. (1-2-3)

(12) Continuous-improvement plans address the processes that directly impact SA issues. (1-2-3)

(13) The day-to-day work of the district attempts to address SA issues. (1-2-3)

(14) The school or district's programs address SA issues. (1-2-3)

(15) The leadership regularly communicates the importance of SA issues. (1-2-3)

(16) The leadership has proposed solutions to the SA issues. (1-2-3)

(17) The proposed solutions are effective. (1-2-3)

(18) The solutions are embedded in the fabric of the organization. (1-2-3)

(19) The organization's processes focus on addressing SA issues. (1-2-3)

(20) The expectations and beliefs of the organization express an ability to overcome SA issues. (1-2-3)

(21) The district identifies indicators or benchmarks to determine progress in meeting its goal(s). (1-2-3)

(22) The organization is inclusive and collaborative in solving SA issues. (1-2-3)

(23) The organization empowers staff in solving identified SA problems. (1-2-3)

(24) The district has identified indicators for high performance. (1-2-3)

Subtotal ____

Atmosphere/Attitude

(1) The organization ensures that all staff members possess and demonstrate the shared values of the organization. (1-2-3)

(2) The school or district encourages professional collaboration. (1-2-3)

(3) Adequate time has been provided for professional collaboration. (1-2-3)

(4) Training has been provided for problem solving. (1-2-3)

(5) Practices and processes empower staff. (1-2-3)

(6) The organization recruits new staff with the necessary attitude, personality, and aptitude aligning with the vision of the district. (1-2-3)

(7) The district recruits new staff with skills that align with its goals. (1-2-3)

(8) The district places staff in positions based on their strengths. (1-2-3)

(9)   The district has the "right people on the bus."   (1-2-3)

(10) The district ensures that members are working toward the common   (1-2-3)
      goals of the organization

(11) The district is a team, with all members working toward a common   (1-2-3)
      goal.

(12) There is a strong sense of collaboration, buy-in, and inclusion.   (1-2-3)

(13) The district fosters a strong mentoring/coaching model for staff.   (1-2-3)

(14) The district supports a tiered professional-development plan.   (1-2-3)

(15) The district supports a teacher-leader program.   (1-2-3)

(16) The district supports a career ladder to support teachers who are   (1-2-3)
      interested in greater leadership opportunities.

(17) Members of the organization feel they are recognized for their   (1-2-3)
      performance.

(18) All members of the organization collaborate to improve practices and processes. (1-2-3)

(19) The district encourages each professional to develop his or her skills and to improve. (1-2-3)

(20) District employees can acquire what is needed to be successful. (1-2-3)

Subtotal ____

Accountability

(1) The district regularly meets its targeted outcomes. (1-2-3)

(2) The district values individual accountability at all levels. (1-2-3)

(3) The district values collective or group accountability. (1-2-3)

(4) The district's system of accountability motivates me. (1-2-3)

(5) The district has a system-wide program of assessment to collect, (1-2-3)
     organize, analyze, and monitor data.

(6) The data gathering focuses on student achievement. (1-2-3)

(7) The district provides a design for the development of goals at the (1-2-3)
     elementary, middle, and high school levels.

(8) District goals and expectations are clearly and consistently (1-2-3)
     communicated.

(9) Building goals are formulated from district goals. (1-2-3)

(10) All goals have a defined method of measurement. (1-2-3)

(11) Action plans are spin-offs of district goals. (1-2-3)

(12) The district utilizes multiple sources of data, benchmarks, and (1-2-3)
     indicators of success in its analysis of student achievement.

(13) The district regularly reviews data outcomes. (1-2-3)

(14) Data reviews are collaborative with and transparent to staff. (1-2-3)

(15) The district utilizes data to make adjustments in the instructional or operational processes immediately. (1-2-3)

(16) The accountability system effectively links curriculum, instruction, and assessment outcomes. (1-2-3)

(17) The accountability system includes classroom goals. (1-2-3)

(18) The accountability system encourages classroom-action research. (1-2-3)

(19) The accountability system supports struggling staff members. (1-2-3)

(20) The accountability system supports professional growth and promotes leadership. (1-2-3)

(21) Members of the organization are proficient in measuring student achievement. (1-2-3)

(22) Members of the organization are proficient in analyzing and utilizing data. (1-2-3)

(23) The district's data warehouse links student reports, data, and teacher planning supports. (1-2-3)

(24) The organization views accountability both collectively and individually. (1-2-3)

(25) Summative evaluations are perceived as fair and equitable. (1-2-3)

Subtotal ____

Adept Leadership for the Twenty-First Century

(1) The leadership was integral in the goal-development process. (1-2-3)

(2) The leadership reviewed final action goals. (1-2-3)

(3) The leadership steps up and provides direction in reinforcing the beliefs and values of the organization. (1-2-3)

(4) The leadership eliminates marginal and unproductive programs. (1-2-3)

(5) The leadership eliminates noninstructional distractions. (1-2-3)

(6) The leadership is laser-focused on achievement and improvement. (1-2-3)

(7) The leadership utilizes practical and visionary judgment in moving the district both vertically and horizontally toward its goals. (1-2-3)

(8) The leadership is flexible in the action-plan-implementation process. (1-2-3)

(9) The leadership is inclusive in the decision-making process. (1-2-3)

(10) The leadership encourages risk-taking or out-of-the-box thinking. (1-2-3)

(11) The leadership engages all stakeholders in the mission of the organization. (1-2-3)

(12) The leadership seeks outside resources to assist with its mission. (1-2-3)

(13) The leadership reinforces teamwork to reach the organization's goals. (1-2-3)

(14) The leadership values the people in its organization. (1-2-3)

(15) The leadership helps its staff grow professionally. (1-2-3)

(16) The leadership is inclusive in its ability to resolve complex issues. (1-2-3)

(17) The leadership effectively communicates with all staff members. (1-2-3)

(18) The leadership effectively models the values, beliefs, and mission of the organization. (1-2-3)

(19) The leadership has effectively organized all instructional and noninstructional structures and processes for success. (1-2-3)

(20) The leadership assumes responsibility for the success or shortcomings of the district. (1-2-3)

(21) The leadership has the expertise to execute goals successfully and achieve high levels of performance. (1-2-3)

(22) The leadership has developed a well-articulated parent- and community-engagement program. (1-2-3)

(23) The leadership creates an environment in which students and staff are empowered to succeed. (1-2-3)

(24) The leadership team operates in a fair, equitable, and professional manner. (1-2-3)

(25) The leadership recognizes staff accomplishments. (1-2-3)

Subtotal ____

Scoring

Alignment ____

Atmosphere/attitude ____

Accountability ____

Adept leadership ____

PART 2, DOCUMENT REVIEW AND ANALYSIS (OPTIONAL)

The document-review component of the cross-check instrument examines and further analyzes the impact of school or district policies regarding student achievement and school or district effectiveness in the context of the four elements—alignment, atmosphere/attitude, accountability, and adept leadership. The documents reviewed are listed in the following areas:

Strategic plans/school and district goals
Human-resources recruitment and hiring
Curriculum and programming
Instructional practices and methodology
System of assessment and achievement data
Observation/supervision and evaluation practices
Professional development
Financial planning: Priorities and allocations
Communication plan
Board policies

Document Review: Ratings and Criteria

INSTRUCTIONS: Rate the designated areas based on the following rubric.

3

Documents and plans reflect current district strategic planning and thinking.
Organizational documents align with organizational outcomes.
Processes and practices are consistent with targeted goals and outcomes.
The mission, vision, values, and beliefs are embedded.
Best practices are represented in all documents, policies, and practices.
Policies and practices contribute to an environment of continuous improvement.
An optimum learning environment is a result of quality practices and policies.
Policies contribute to organizational effectiveness.
Policies, practices, and documents reflect a professional environment.

2

Documents and plans are inconsistent in reflecting current district strategic planning and thinking.
Organizational documents sporadically align with organizational outcomes.

Processes and practices are inconsistent with targeted goals and outcomes.

The mission, vision, values, and beliefs are periodically mentioned in documents.

Best practices are somewhat represented in documents, practices, and policies.

The documents, practices, and policies may contribute to continuous improvement.

The learning environment is less than ideal.

Policies contributing to organizational effectiveness are not consistent in all areas.

The professional environment is hindered by the district's practices and policies.

1

Documents and plans do not reflect current district strategic planning and thinking.

Organizational documents do not align with organizational outcomes.

Processes and practices do not target desired goals and outcomes.

The mission, vision, values, and belief statements are not represented in documents.

There is no evidence of best practices in documents, policies, and practices.

An environment of continuous improvement is nonexistent.

The learning environment is poor.

Policies do not contribute to organizational effectiveness.

A professional learning environment is nonexistent.

Summative Document Ratings

Document Review: Notations

School or district:

Name of document:

Descriptors

Strategic planning
Organizational outcomes
Processes/practices
Vision, values, beliefs

(1)	Strategic plans/school and district goals	1-2-3
(2)	Human-resources recruitment and hiring	1-2-3
(3)	Curriculum and programming	1-2-3
(4)	Instructional practices and methodology	1-2-3
(5)	System of assessment and achievement data	1-2-3
(6)	Observation/supervision and evaluation practices	1-2-3
(7)	Professional development	1-2-3
(8)	Financial: budget review/priorities/allocations	1-2-3
(9)	Communication plan	1-2-3
(10)	Board policies	1-2-3

Total score ____

Conclusion (see separate report, attached.)

Recommendation (see separate report, attached.)

Best practices
Learning environment
Organizational effectiveness
Professional environment

Appendix C

My One-Page Plan

Our administrative team was adamant that our newly developed strategic plan would be utilized to guide the direction of the district. Unlike state requirements, which only focuses on the academic side of the organization, our team sought to utilize the plan to guide every operational facet and department of our school district because we recognized that an alignment of all employee groups would laser focus the district on high expectations and improved outcomes.

We wanted to implement a comprehensive and aligned plan that would clearly communicate the district's priorities and ensure that all employees understood that they are working toward a set of common goals and one in which data would be utilized to determine progress. Without such a plan it was recognized that the district would not be effective in implementing a continuous-improvement model.

We also recognized that the success or failure of such a plan was tied directly to creating an atmosphere of collaboration in which employee perspectives are valued and their participation in the action components of the plan will impact achievement outcomes. The board clearly communicated that funding was contingent on effectiveness and results.

My One-Page Plan focuses on the implementation process of an improvement plan and on how to make it a living, breathing document.

To ensure that the plan would actually drive the work of the district on a day-to-day basis, each member of the organization had to contribute to achieving the established goals in an equitable manner and feel that their work is making a difference in reaching the goal of world-class outcomes. After years of developing goals that never seemed to deliver the designated outcomes, we wanted to infuse an accountability system into the improvement process to not only chart and monitor growth but also assist those in attempting to meet those goals. To accomplish this task, My One-Page Plan was the answer.

As superintendent, I found that previous action plans had basically been maintained in a large notebook. While I had at my fingertips a listing of all the proposed action plans, this method for implementation was both cumbersome and ineffective. Too many times either the reporting process was vague or not current and so yielded information of little significance.

Rather, My One-Page Plan, an online planning tool, ensures that planning "is a continuous process . . . not just an event." This tool enabled me to view progress on a weekly or monthly basis and review how each administrator was attempting to meet those goals. This accountability process assisted in building a foundation of alignment that cascaded throughout each department and organization.

Often many senior leaders believe that their role is simply limited to overseeing and monitoring, but in reality a more active role is necessary. Active leadership requires that administrators lead meetings with departments and other groups to understand the ongoing work. In these meetings administrators recognize the personnel carrying out those goals and provide support and resources to staff as they move the goals forward into the classroom.

If they're doing their jobs correctly, the senior leadership team recognizes that each initiative and goal is not completed in isolation. For example, implementing a technology goal should include input and assistance from facilities, curriculum, and financial departments along with input at the building level. The senior leadership, therefore, assumes responsibility for the facilitation and orchestration of the goal and associated activities from the beginning until completion.

Key action steps ensure that the action plans are developed in a consistent manner. These steps are measurable and specify the leadership actions necessary to a successful completion of the goal. The process includes:

- regular monthly online updates
- actions for which each leader is responsible
- actions steps that include a description
- and accountability, including specification of responsible staff, dates, and documented evidence for completion.

From my perspective, My One-Page Plan works because the superintendent can continually review progress and the associated data to keep the organization moving toward the targeted goal. Since the plan includes the vision, mission, measurable objectives, strategies, and action plans, the process truly aligns the organization in a collaborative manner with the designated goals. This alignment not only provides a foundation for excellence but its operational execution.

The superintendent's role in the district is not just to be a visionary. The role requires more than a cursory oversight or simply completing the "administrivia" that is a required component of the position. The role requires more than leading members of the board of education. Successful outcomes require a superintendent with the aptitude to acknowledge that their role is to ensure alignment, goal deployment, and execution. This role requires someone who knows how to engage staff in a collaborative and positive manner. Most importantly, a twenty-first-century superintendent leader does not stand on the sidelines but rather is actively engaged in building an environment that aligns the organization in a synergistic manner that harnesses its collective strength to reach world-class outcomes.

Appendix D

Master-Teacher Program

CRITERIA AND APPLICATION PROCESS

I. Criteria

    a. Advanced professional certificate
    b. Evaluation

- Satisfactory final ratings in all categories (five consecutive years)
- No minimum performance ratings (last five years)

    c. Classroom action research planning and goals (minimum one year)
    d. Leadership

- Committee participation: building or district level
- Conference and workshop attendance
- Curriculum writing and implementation
- Formal and informal mentoring of teachers
- Demonstration lessons of best practices

II. Application Process

    a. Submission of cover application
    b. Supplemental information

- Classroom action research plans, goals, and outcomes
- Principal recommendation
- Observation reports (five consecutive years)

- Written response: Describe why you are a master-teacher (refer to skills and knowledge standards rubric*)
- Teach a demonstration lesson to representatives of the master-teacher committee

III. Submission

   a. Submit the application and requested information in a binder to the superintendent of schools for review.
   b. Organize binder as follows:

   - Principal recommendations
   - Last five years of final evaluations
   - Actions research project
   - Summary of leadership in the district (define your role, contribution, etc.)

   c. Plan a model lesson with all key components
   d. Observation reports (five years)
   e. Written response (describe why you are a master-teacher)
   f. Demonstration lesson: committee scheduled

IV. Disputes

- All issues regarding the application process will be resolved by the district improvement team prior to formal submission of the application to the superintendent
- Selection: recommendation by the master-teacher committee, superintendent will make the final decision, all decisions are final

---

*Master-teacher program authored by Dr. Vincent F. Cotter as superintendent of the Colonial School District in Plymouth Meeting, Pennsylvania, 2001.

Notes

INTRODUCTION

1. US Department of Education, "Race to the Top Executive Summary," *ED Recovery Act: American Recovery and Reinvestment of 2009* (Washington, DC: 2009) http://www.nces.ed.gov/.
2. Eric A. Hanushek, Paul E. Peterson, and Ludger Woessmann, *Endangering Prosperity: A Global View of the American School*, foreword by Lawrence H. Summers (Washington, DC: Brookings Institution Press. 2013).
3. Douglas B. Reeves, "The Learning Leader: How to Focus Improvement for Better Results," ASCD, 2006, p. 80.
4. Lawrence W. Lezotte, "Leadership for the Journey Ahead," lecture, twenty-fourth annual Effective Schools Conference, Fort Washington, PA, November 2006.
5. Jim Collins, *Good to Great: Why Some Companies Make the Leap . . . and Others Don't* (New York: HarperCollins Publishers, 2001), 1.
6. Ronald Edmonds, "Effective Schools for the Urban Poor," *Educational Leadership* 37, no. 1 (October 1979): 23–24, archived online at http://www.ascd.org/ASCD/pdf/journals/ed_lead/el_197910_edmonds.pdf.
7. Hanushek, Peterson, and Woessmann, *Endangering Prosperity*, 11–12.

1. ALIGNMENT

1. David Anspaugh, dir., *Hoosiers* (Los Angeles: Orion Pictures, 1986).
2. See Thomas J. Peters and Robert H. Waterman, *In Search of Excellence: Lessons from America's Best-Run Companies* (New York: HarperCollins, 2006). And see Jim Collins, *Good to Great: Why Some Companies Make the Leap . . . and Others Don't* (New York: HarperCollins Publishers, 2001).
3. Elizabeth Mann, "School Turnaround under ESSA: Progress, but Not a Silver Bullet," *The Brown Center Chalkboard* (blog), Brookings Institute, October 31, 2016, https://www.brookings.edu/blog/brown-center-chalkboard/2016/10/31/school-turnaround-under-essa-progress-but-not-a-silver-bullet/.

2. AN ACHIEVEMENT-FOCUSED ATTITUDE

1. *The Hechinger Report*, "Why School Leadership Matters," Teachers College, Columbia University, March 3, 2011, http://hechingerreport.org/why-school-leadership-matters/.
2. David Brown, Josh Bersin, Will Gosling, and Nathan Sloan, "Engagement Always On," *Global Human Capital Trends 2016*, Deloitte University Press report, February 29, 2016, p. 9, https://dupress.deloitte.com/dup-us-en/focus/human-capital-trends/2016/employee-engagement-and-retention.html.
3. Susan Sorenson, "How Employee Engagement Drives Growth," *Gallup Business Journal*, June 20, 2013, http://news.gallup.com/businessjournal/163130/employee-engagement-drives-growth.aspx.
4. J. McPherson and B. Jayatilleke, *Culture Amp: New Tech Benchmark Report 2016* ([Melbourne, AUS]: Culture Amp, 2016), 13.
5. Eric Prisbell, "The Revival of Texas Basketball and Coach Rick Barnes," *USA Today*, February 6, 2014, pp. 1–5, https://www.usatoday.com/story/sports/ncaab/big12/2014/02/06/university-of-texas-longhorns-basketball-coach-rick-barnes/5264209/.
6. Scott Beare and Michael McMillan, *The Power of Teamwork* (Naperville, IL: Simple Truths, 2006), 54–55, 16–30.
7. Ibid., 45.

3. ACCOUNTABILITY

1. Dale Mezzacappa, "Teaching Evaluation System has Lots of Critics," http://thenotebook.org/articles/2009/05/27/teacher-evaluation-system-has-lots-of-critics, p. 1.
2. Jim Horan, *The One Page Business Plan* (Berkeley: The One Page Business Plan Co., 2007), 29.
3. Drawn from Horan, *The One Page Plan*.
4. William L. Sanders and June C. Rivers, *Cumulative and Residual Effects of Teachers on Future Student Academic Achievement* (Knoxville: University of Tennessee Value-Added Research and Assessment Center, 1996), pp. 6–7, archived online at http://www.cgp.upenn.edu/pdf/Sanders_Rivers-TVASS_teacher effects.pdf.
5. Pamela D. Tucker and James H. Stronge, *Linking Teacher Evaluation and Student Learning* (Alexandria, VA: Association for Supervision and Curriculum Development, 2005), 4.
6. Sanders and Rivers, *Cumulative and Residual Effects*, 6.
7. Peter Mortimore and Pam Sammons, "New Evidence on Effective Elementary Schools," *Educational Leadership* 45, no. 1 (September 1987): 4–8, http://ascd.com/ASCD/pdf/journals/ed_lead/el_198709_mortimore.pdf.
8. Thomas J. Kane, Eric S. Taylor, John H. Tyler, and Amy L. Wooten, "Identifying Effective Classroom Practices Using Student Achievement Data," National Bureau of Economic Research Working Paper Series, #15803, Cambridge, MA, March 2010, p. 59, http://www.nber.org/papers/w15803.pdf.

4. APTITUDE FOR ADEPT LEADERSHIP

1. Jennifer Parker, "Duncan Faces Political Battle Over Education Reform," ABC News, June 19, 2009, http://abcnews.go.com/ThisWeek/Politics/story?id=7876217.

2. Mike Schmoker, *The Results Fieldbook: Practical Strategies from Dramatically Improved Schools* (Alexandria, VA: Association for Supervision and Curriculum Development, 2001), 121.

3. Peter Block, "Consortium for Educational Change," lecture, Summer Institute, 1988 in John G. Conyers and Robert Ewy, *Charting Your Course: Lessons Learned during the Journey toward Performance Excellence* (Milwaukee: ASQ Quality Press, 2004).

4. Joseph A. Michelli, *The New Gold Standard: 5 Leadership Principles for Creating a Legendary Customer Experience Courtesy of the Ritz-Carlton Hotel Company*. (New York: McGraw-Hill, 2008), 24.

5. Larry Bossidy and Ram Charan, *Execution: The Discipline of Getting Things Done* (New York: Crown Business, 2002), 6.

6. Robert K. Greenleaf Center for Servant Leadership, "Start Here: What Is Servant Leadership?" accessed April 21, 2017, https://www.greenleaf.org/what-is-servant-leadership/.

7. Sam Tyler, dir., *Creating a People-Centered Organization*, DVD (Cambridge, MA: Enterprise Media, 1999).

8. Collins, *Good to Great*, 11–12; John G. Conyers and Robert Ewy, *Charting Your Course: Lessons Learned during the Journey toward Performance Excellence* (Milwaukee: ASQ Quality Press, 2004).

9. Kenneth H. Blanchard, John P. Carlos, and W. Alan Randolph, *The 3 Keys to Empowerment: Release the Power within People for Astonishing Results*, 2nd ed. (San Francisco: Berrett-Koehler, 2001), 2.

10. Ralph Smith, "Grade-Level Reading: Tackling Our Greatest Education Challenge," lecture, Herald Tribune Media Group Community Forum, jointly sponsored by Manatee and Sarasota County School Districts, Sarasota, FL, June 2015.

11. John G. Conyers and Robert Ewy, *Charting Your Course: Lessons Learned during the Journey toward Performance Excellence* (Milwaukee: ASQ Quality Press, 2004), 3c.

12. Erika Andersen, "Are Leaders Born or Made?" Forbes (blog), November 21, 2012, https://www.forbes.com/sites/erikaandersen/2012/11/21/are-leaders-born-or-made/.

5. ORGANIZATIONAL REFLECTION

1. Brooke Singman, "Education Department Report Finds Billions Spent under Obama Had 'No Impact' on Achievement," Fox News Politics (blog), January 25, 2017, http://www.foxnews.com/politics/2017/01/25/education-department-report-finds-billions-spent-under-obama-had-no-impact-on-achievement.html.

2. David Leonhardt, "Schools That Work," Sunday Review, *New York Times*, November 4, 2016, https://www.nytimes.com/2016/11/06/opinion/sunday/schools-that-work.html.

3. Reeves, "The Learning Leader: How to Focus Improvement for Better Results," ASCD, 2006.

6. MAKING SCHOOLS AND DISTRICTS HIGH PERFORMING

1. Julia Terruso, "A $24,000 Question: Camden's per Pupil Funding Not Whole Story," *Philadelphia Inquirer*, April 13, 2014, B01.

2. Dale Mezzacappa, "High School 2.0," Education Next 10, no. 2 (Spring 2010): 1, http://educationnext.org/high-school-2-0/.

3. ABC News, "Inside Google's Culture and Leadership New Book Tells 'How Google Works,'" Rebecca Jarvis interviewing Eric Schmidt and Jonathan Rosenberg on *Real Biz*,

filmed September 2014, http://abcnews.go.com/Business/video/inside-googles-culture-leadership-book-tells-google-works-25701847.

4. Charles Darwin, *On the Origin of Species: By Means of Natural Selection; or, the Preservation of Favoured Races in the Struggle for Life* (London: John Murray, 1859).

5. John P. Kotter and Holger Rathgeber, *Our Iceberg Is Melting* (New York: St. Martin's Press, 2005), 3–5.

6. Edward Tylor, "The Definition of Culture." *Popular Science Monthly* 26 (1884): 145.

7. Robert M. Gates, *Duty: Memoirs of a Secretary at War* (New York: Alfred A. Knopf, 2014), 83.

8. M. Night Shyamalan, "He Got Schooled: M. Night Shyamalan on Closing the Education Gap," Q&A with Tess Vigeland, 88.9 KPCC Radio, Southern California Public Radio, with Ana Ponce, Pasadena, CA, January 13, 2014, archived online at https://www.youtube.com/watch?v=LQj9364kNKM.

9. Hanushek, Peterson, and Woessmann, *Endangering Prosperity*, 11.

10. Bossidy and Charan, *Execution*, 19.

11. Hanushek, Peterson, and Woessmann, *Endangering Prosperity*, 10.

7. PLANNING FOR SUCCESS

1. Lawrence W. Lezotte and Barbara C. Jacoby, *Sustainable School Reform: The District Context for School Improvement* (Okemos, MI: Effective Schools Products, 1991), 238–45.

8. STRATEGIES FOR SUCCESS

1. Bossidy and Charan, *Execution*, 6.

2. Robert K. Greenleaf Center for Servant Leadership, "Start Here."

3. Learn more about the Fish! Philosophy at ChartHouse Learning's website, http://www.fishphilosophy.com.

9. CASE STUDIES

1. Bossidy and Charan, *Execution*, 184, 70, and 71.

CONCLUSION

1. Lezotte, "Leadership for the Journey Ahead."

2. National Center for Educational Statistics, "Fast Facts: Education Statistics," n.d., https://nces.ed.gov/fastfacts/display.asp?id=372.

3. National Assessment of Educational Progress, "National Assessment of Educational Progress (NAEP): Nations Report Card," Washington, D.C., last modified 2015, https://nces.ed.gov/nationsreportcard2015/.

4. Ibid.

5. Mark Dynarski, "Teacher Observations Have Been a Waste of Time and Money," Brookings Institute, report, December 8, 2016, pp. 1–10, https://www.brookings.edu/research/teacher-observations-have-been-a-waste-of-time-and-money/.

6. National Commission on Excellence in Education, *A Nation at Risk: The Imperative for Educational Reform* (Washington, DC: US Government Printing Office, 1983), http://files.eric.ed.gov/fulltext/ED226006.pdf.

7. Mann, "School Turnaround under ESSA."

8. Stanley McChrystal, *Team of Teams: New Rules of Engagement for a Complex World*, with Tatum Collins, David Silverman, and Chris Fussell (London: Penguin Random House, 2015).

9. Lezotte and Jacoby, *Sustainable School Reform*.

Bibliography

ABC News. "Inside Google's Culture and Leadership New Book Tells 'How Google Works.'" Rebecca Jarvis interviewing Eric Schmidt and Jonathan Rosenberg on *Real Biz*, filmed September 2014. http://abcnews.go.com/Business/video/inside-googles-culture-leadership-book-tells-google-works-25701847.
Andersen, Erika. "Are Leaders Born or Made?" Forbes (blog), November 21, 2012. https://www.forbes.com/sites/erikaandersen/2012/11/21/are-leaders-born-or-made/.
Anspaugh, David, dir. *Hoosiers*. Los Angeles: Orion Pictures, 1986.
Beare, Scott, and Michael McMillan. *The Power of Teamwork*. Naperville, IL: Simple Truths, 2006.
Blanchard, Kenneth H., John P. Carlos, and W. Alan Randolph. *The 3 Keys to Empowerment: Release the Power within People for Astonishing Results*, 2nd ed. San Francisco: Berrett-Koehler, 2001.
Block, Peter. "Consortium for Educational Change." Lecture, Summer Institute, 1988.
Bossidy, Larry, and Ram Charan. *Execution: The Discipline of Getting Things Done*. New York: Crown Business, 2002.
Brown, David, Josh Bersin, Will Gosling, and Nathan Sloan. "Engagement Always On." *Global Human Capital Trends 2016*. Deloitte University Press report. February 29, 2016. https://dupress.deloitte.com/dup-us-en/focus/human-capital-trends/2016/employee-engagement-and-retention.html.
Coleman, James S., Ernest Q. Campbell, Carol J. Hobson, James McPartland, Alexander M. Mood, Frederic D. Weinfeld, and Robert L. York. Equality of Educational Opportunity. National Center for Educational Statistics, US Department of Health, Education, and Welfare, Office of Education. Washington, DC: US Government Printing Office, 1966. Archived at http://files.eric.ed.gov/fulltext/ED012275.pdf.
Collins, Jim. *Good to Great: Why Some Companies Make the Leap . . . and Others Don't*. New York: HarperCollins Publishers, 2001.
Conyers, John G., and Robert Ewy. *Charting Your Course: Lessons Learned during the Journey toward Performance Excellence*. Milwaukee: ASQ Quality Press, 2004.
Covey, Stephen R. *The 8th Habit: From Effectiveness to Greatness*. New York: Free Press, 2005.
Darwin, Charles. *On the Origin of Species: By Means of Natural Selection; or, the Preservation of Favoured Races in the Struggle for Life*. London: John Murray, 1859.
Dynarski, Mark. "Teacher Observations Have Been a Waste of Time and Money." Brookings Institute, report. December 8, 2016. https://www.brookings.edu/research/teacher-observations-have-been-a-waste-of-time-and-money/.

Edmonds, Ronald. "Effective Schools for the Urban Poor." *Educational Leadership* 37, no. 1 (October 1979): 15–24. Archived online at http://www.ascd.org/ASCD/pdf/journals/ed_lead/el_197910_edmonds.pdf.

Gates, Robert M. Duty: *Memoirs of a Secretary at War*. New York: Alfred A. Knopf, 2014.

Hanushek, Eric A., Paul E. Peterson, and Ludger Woessmann. *Endangering Prosperity: A Global View of the American School*. Foreword by Lawrence H. Summers. Washington, DC: Brookings Institution Press. 2013.

The Hechinger Report. "Why School Leadership Matters." Teachers College, Columbia University. March 3, 2011. http://hechingerreport.org/why-school-leadership-matters/.

Horan, Jim. *The One Page Business Plan: Start with a Vision, Build a Company!* and *The One Page Business Plan: The Fastest, Easiest Way to Write a Business Plan*. Berkeley, CA: The One Page Business Plan Company, 1998/2007.

Johnson, W. Brad, and Gregory P. Harper. *Becoming a Leader the Annapolis Way: 12 Combat Lessons from the Navy's Leadership Laboratory*. New York: McGraw-Hill, 2004.

Kane, Thomas J., Eric S. Taylor, John H. Tyler, and Amy L. Wooten. "Identifying Effective Classroom Practices Using Student Achievement Data." National Bureau of Economic Research Working Paper Series, #15803, Cambridge, MA, March 2010. http://www.nber.org/papers/w15803.pdf.

Kotter, John P., and Holger Rathgeber. *Our Iceberg Is Melting*. New York: St. Martin's Press, 2005.

Leonhardt, David. "Schools That Work." Sunday Review, *New York Times*, November 4, 2016. https://www.nytimes.com/2016/11/06/opinion/sunday/schools-that-work.html.

Levitan, Daniel. "The Original Mind: Thinking Straight in an Age of Information Overload." Talks at Google, October 28, 2014. http://www.YouTube.com.

Lezotte, Lawrence W. "Leadership for the Journey Ahead." Lecture, twenty-fourth annual Effective Schools Conference, Fort Washington, PA, November 2006.

Lezotte, Lawrence W., and Barbara C. Jacoby. *Sustainable School Reform: The District Context for School Improvement*. Okemos, MI: Effective Schools Products, 1991.

Mann, Elizabeth. "School Turnaround under ESSA: Progress, but Not a Silver Bullet." *The Brown Center Chalkboard* (blog). Brookings Institute. October 31, 2016. https://www.brookings.edu/blog/brown-center-chalkboard/2016/10/31/school-turnaround-under-essa-progress-but-not-a-silver-bullet/.

McChrystal, Stanley, Tatum Collins, David Silverman, and Chris Fussell. *Team of Teams: New Rules of Engagement for a Complex World*. London: Penguin Random House, 2015.

McPherson, J., and B. Jayatilleke. *Culture Amp: New Tech Benchmark Report 2016*. [Melbourne, AUS]: Culture Amp, 2016, 13.

Mezzacappa, Dale. "High School 2.0." *Education Next* 10, no. 2 (Spring 2010). http://educationnext.org/high-school-2-0/.

Mezzacappa, Dale. "Teacher Evaluation System Has Lots of Critics." http://www.thenotebook.org/articles/05/27/2009, p. 1.

Michelli, Joseph A. *The New Gold Standard: 5 Leadership Principles for Creating a Legendary Customer Experience Courtesy of the Ritz-Carlton Hotel Company*. New York: McGraw-Hill, 2008.

Mortimore, Peter, and Pam Sammons. "New Evidence on Effective Elementary Schools." *Educational Leadership* 45, no. 1 (September 1987): 4–8. http://ascd.com/ASCD/pdf/journals/ed_lead/el_198709_mortimore.pdf.

National Assessment of Educational Progress. "National Assessment of Educational Progress (NAEP): Nations Report Card." Washington, DC. Last modified 2015. https://nces.ed.gov/nationsreportcard2015/.

National Center for Educational Statistics. "Fast Facts: Education Statistics." n.d. https://nces.ed.gov/fastfacts/display.asp?id=372.

National Commission on Excellence in Education. *A Nation at Risk: The Imperative for Educational Reform*. Washington, DC: US Government Printing Office, 1983. http://files.eric.ed.gov/fulltext/ED226006.pdf.

Parker, Jennifer. "Duncan Faces Political Battle Over Education Reform." ABC News. June 19, 2009. http://abcnews.go.com/ThisWeek/Politics/story?id=7876217.

Peters, Thomas J., and Robert H. Waterman. *In Search of Excellence: Lessons from America's Best-Run Companies*. New York: HarperCollins, 2006.

Prisbell, Eric. "The Revival of Texas Basketball and Coach Rick Barnes." *USA Today*. February 6, 2014. https://www.usatoday.com/story/sports/ncaab/big12/2014/02/06/university-of-texas-longhorns-basketball-coach-rick-barnes/5264209/.

Reeves, Douglas. "The Learning Leader: How to Focus Improvement for Better Results." ASCD, 2006, p. 80.

Robert K. Greenleaf Center for Servant Leadership. "Start Here: What Is Servant Leadership?" Accessed April 21, 2017. https://www.greenleaf.org/what-is-servant-leadership/.

Sanders, William L., and June C. Rivers. *Cumulative and Residual Effects of Teachers on Future Student Academic Achievement*. Knoxville: University of Tennessee Value-Added Research and Assessment Center, 1996. Archived online at http://www.cgp.upenn.edu/pdf/Sanders_Rivers-TVASS_teacher effects.pdf.

Schmoker, Mike. *The Results Fieldbook: Practical Strategies from Dramatically Improved Schools*. Alexandria, VA: Association for Supervision and Curriculum Development, 2001.

Shyamalan, M. Night. "He Got Schooled: M. Night Shyamalan on Closing the Education Gap." Q&A with Tess Vigeland. 88.9 KPCC Radio, Southern California Public Radio. With Ana Ponce. Pasadena, CA, January 13, 2014. Archived online at https://www.youtube.com/watch?v=LQj9364kNKM.

Singman, Brooke. "Education Department Report Finds Billions Spent under Obama Had 'No Impact' on Achievement." Fox News Politics (blog). January 25, 2017. http://www.foxnews.com/politics/2017/01/25/education-department-report-finds-billions-spent-under-obama-had-no-impact-on-achievement.html.

Smith, Ralph. "Grade-Level Reading: Tackling Our Greatest Education Challenge." Lecture, Herald Tribune Media Group Community Forum, jointly sponsored by Manatee and Sarasota County School Districts, Sarasota, FL, June 2015.

Sorenson, Susan. "How Employee Engagement Drives Growth." *Gallup Business Journal*, June 20, 2013. http://news.gallup.com/businessjournal/163130/employee-engagement-drives-growth.aspx.

Terruso, Julia. "A $24,000 Question: Camden's per Pupil Funding Not Whole Story." *Philadelphia Inquirer*, April 13, 2014, B01.

Tucker, Pamela D., and James H. Stronge. *Linking Teacher Evaluation and Student Learning*. Alexandria, VA: Association for Supervision and Curriculum Development, 2005.

Tyler, Sam, dir. *Creating a People-Centered Organization*. DVD. Cambridge, MA: Enterprise Media, 1999.

Tylor, Edward. "The Definition of Culture." *Popular Science Monthly* 26 (1884): 145.

US Department of Education. "Race to the Top Executive Summary" Washington, DC: Department of Education, 2009, p. 2.

About the Authors

With over forty years in the field of education, Dr. **Vincent F. Cotter**, EdD, served as teacher, department chair, and administrator in both urban and urban-suburban public school environments. As superintendent of schools for eleven consecutive years, he was the primary innovator of a unique program, Reaching Above and Beyond, which dramatically improved student achievement. For his efforts, Dr. Cotter was awarded the prestigious American Society for Quality's international Juran Medal (2010) in the field of education, for sustained systemic improvement. Dr. Cotter has also written graduate-level courses for aspiring principals and superintendents, provided consultative services to school districts, and cofounded the Exemplary Schools Organization.

As a career educator for over thirty-five years, Dr. **Robert D. Hassler**, EdD, served as an elementary- and middle-school teacher, director of curriculum, and assistant superintendent in several school districts. During his tenure as superintendent, Dr. Hassler spearheaded the implementation of various continuous improvement efforts that resulted in over ten consecutive years of increases in student achievement, increased participation in advanced-placement courses by over 200 percent and provided leadership in closing the achievement gap for all student subgroups. Under his leadership the district also received numerous state and national academic and communication awards and was recognized for various parent- and community-engagement and student-activities programs. Currently Dr. Hassler is an independent consultant in the field and is cofounder of the Exemplary Schools Organization.

www.ingramcontent.com/pod-product-compliance
Lightning Source LLC
Chambersburg PA
CBHW030113010526
44116CB00005B/230